CHARACTER
COUNTS

THE POWER OF PERSONAL INTEGRITY

CHARLES H. DYER

MOODY PUBLISHERS

CHICAGO

Editor: Pam Pugh
Interior Design: Ragont Design
Cover Design: Smartt Guys design
Cover Photo: Gail Johnson / Dreamstime

Library of Congress Cataloging-in-Publication Data

Dyer, Charles H.
Character counts : the power of personal integrity / by Charles H. Dyer.
   p. cm.
Includes bibliographical references (p.   ).
ISBN 978-0-8024-3909-3
1. Integrity—Religious aspects—Christianity. I. Title.
BV4647.I55.D83 2010
241'.4—dc22
                                    2009037126

This book is printed on acid free recycled paper containing 30% PCW (Post Consumer Waste) and manufactured in the United States of America by Versa Press.

We hope you enjoy this book from Moody Publishers. Our goal is to provide high-quality, thought-provoking books and products that connect truth to your real needs and challenges. For more information on other books and products written and produced from a biblical perspective, go to www.moodypublishers.com or write to:

Moody Publishers
820 N. LaSalle Boulevard
Chicago, IL 60610

1 3 5 7 9 10 8 6 4 2

Printed in the United States of America

This book is dedicated to
Mark Bailey, Doug Cecil, Greg Hatteberg,
Doug Lyon, Walt McCord, and Steve Mills—
six godly men who have each been living examples of
integrity and authenticity in my life for more than twenty years.
It's a privilege to call each of you *friend*.

Faithful are the wounds of a friend,
but deceitful are the kisses of an enemy.
Iron sharpens iron, so one man sharpens another.
Proverbs 27:6, 17

Timothy,

The fear of the is the
beginning of wisdom,
and knowledge of the Holy One
is understanding.

Proverbs 9:10

敬畏耶和華是智慧的開端，
認識至聖者便是聰明。

箴言九章十節

Uncle Raymond
12 December 2010
Edmonton

CONTENTS

FOREWORD

Dr. Karl Menninger once shocked his psychologist colleagues by using the "S" word in the title of his bestseller *Whatever Became of Sin?* For the first time, many of his readers were confronted with a word and a concept that had all but disappeared from their profession.

In a cover story, *Time* magazine asked another probing question, "What Ever Happened to Ethics?" By then, scandals had become the order of the day. They still are. It seems that no place remains sacred any longer; not the Oval Office at the White House or the Pentagon or Capitol Hill or NASA or Wall Street or the sports arena or the halls of academe or the medical and legal professions or, for that matter, the whole world of religion. We have lived through Watergate, Koreagate, Irangate, and even *Pearlygate*, much to the embarrassment of Christians.

The psalmist's words have never been more relevant:

> *"We are objects of reproach to our neighbors,*
> *of scorn and derision to those around us"* (Psalm 79:4).

With the disappearance of sin and the subsequent absence of ethics, no one should be surprised that absolutes of right and wrong have now been replaced by a gray, foggy mixture of uncertainty and inconsistency. Look deep enough, search far enough, stay at it long enough, and skeletons begin to rattle from the closet of most everyone's past. Few are the heroes who can withstand the laserlike probe of today's media examiners. How the mighty are fallen!

What's missing? What do we long to find at the core of those we admire? Integrity. And what is that?

My *Oxford English Dictionary* tells me the word is derived from the Latin *integritas*, which means "wholeness . . . completeness." The root term, *integer*, means "untouched, intact, entire." One with integrity is solid, authentic, upright. Interestingly, the Hebrew term, usually translated "integrity" in the Old Testament (*tome*) means the same thing, "whole, complete, upright, ethically sound."

In light of that, it seems to me what we need most is not more emphasis on the problem but greater insight into the solution. We don't need more heartbreaking stories of scandalous lives but reliable and forthright information on how to live differently in a world that's lost its way. It's time for somebody to answer the real question, "What ever can be done about integrity?"

I have good news! That is precisely what my friend and close personal colleague, Dr. Charles Dyer, has done. In this volume Charlie has not only addressed the need for integrity in a compelling manner, he's also helped us understand its component traits . . . such as honesty, compassion, wisdom, self-control, joy, trust, faithfulness, sexual purity, and other equally significant dimensions of an authentic lifestyle.

I heartily recommend this book! You will find these three essentials here that make it worth your time:

1. It is interesting. You'll be drawn into the stories he tells and the scenes he paints.
2. It is biblical. Again and again, you will return to the Scriptures as a foundation is built and principles are formed.
3. It is resourceful. These pages are not merely the opinion of an author, but helpful, insightful thoughts that add depth to the discussion.

Best of all, the one who writes of integrity has been a consistent model of it for years. I know, having witnessed it over the long haul in situations where it has been put to the test. On each occasion, Charlie Dyer passed with flying colors.

I would make two suggestions before you begin to read. First, from the start, read slowly and carefully. Second, when you finish, ask yourself, "What ever happened to integrity *in me?*"

CHARLES R. SWINDOLL
Chancellor, Dallas Theological Seminary
Bible Teacher, *Insight for Living*

BE MORE CONCERNED WITH YOUR
CHARACTER THAN YOUR REPUTATION,
BECAUSE YOUR CHARACTER IS WHAT
YOU REALLY ARE, WHILE YOUR
REPUTATION IS MERELY WHAT OTHERS
THINK YOU ARE.

—*John Wooden*

EXCELLENCE IS NOT A SINGULAR ACT,
BUT A HABIT. YOU ARE WHAT YOU
REPEATEDLY DO.

—*Shaquille O'Neal*

WHY TALK ABOUT
Character?

Character counts. Ask the thousands of investors who lost their life savings in Bernard Madoff's $65 billion Ponzi scheme . . . the largest investment fraud in history. They put their money—and their trust—in a man who finally admitted his entire operation was "one big lie."[1]

Or ask Jearl Miles-Clark, Monique Hennagan, and La Tasha Colander-Richardson. Don't know them? They were three members of the U.S. 1,600-meter relay team that won gold in the 2000 Sydney Olympics, only to be stripped of their medals in 2008 because the fourth member of that team, Marion Jones, used performance-enhancing drugs. She cheated; they suffered the consequences.

Or ask Scott and Janet Willis, a pastor and his wife who were involved in a tragic crash in Chicago that killed six of their children—a crash caused by a truck driver who had paid a bribe to get his driver's license. The investigation that followed led to the conviction of seventy-five people, including George Ryan, a former governor of Illinois.[2] Those found guilty went to prison, but that brought little comfort to the Willis family.

Character counts, but we often fail to make the connection between character and conduct. Today's headlines highlight society's problems, but then the pundits simplistically push the blame off on big business, big government, or some other faceless entity. Yet—with the exception of natural disasters—most problems are caused by *people* . . . people who put money, power, or personal gain ahead of the bedrock values of character and integrity. Such people act with little regard for the impact their decisions will have on others. I published the first version of this book more than a decade ago[3] in days of unbridled optimism—the economy was booming, housing values were rising, the new frontier of the World Wide Web seemed limitless, and our narcissistic culture didn't care for such antiquated notions as honesty, faithfulness, or self-control. Just show me the money! We are now paying the price for years of selfish excess brought on by such people . . . in business *and* in government.

A recent issue of *Newsweek* featured a stark cover with the title "The Decline and Fall of Christian America."[4] Incredibly, the writer saw a positive benefit to America's becoming less Christian. "While we remain a nation decisively shaped by religious faith, our politics and our culture are, in the main, less influenced by movements and arguments of an explicitly Christian character than they were even five years ago."[5] But is the absence of "Christian character" from our culture a good thing? I think not.

Unfortunately, amid our self-absorbed grab-for-all-the-gusto lifestyle we fail to heed a basic warning from God's Word. "Do not be deceived: God cannot be mocked. A man reaps what he sows" (Galatians 6:7). Now we are experiencing the harvest of our neglect. From our crumbling families . . . to our battered economy . . . to our battle-scarred cities and towns, the price for ignoring issues of character and integrity has been high. It's time to refocus.

This book is about integrity, character, and values. The key qualities needed to live a life of integrity will be explained and illustrated through stories of men and women in the Bible. Conduct reveals character, and we best understand integrity when we see it lived out in a person's life. God understands this principle . . . and that's why so much of the Bible tells God's truth through the lives of people. Want to learn how to be wise? Walk with Solomon through the wise—and foolish—steps of his life. Struggling with faith? Travel in Abraham's caravan and watch his faith take shape and deepen. Concerned that your life is out of balance? Visit the home of Mary and Martha and observe these two women struggle to maintain balance during the stress points of their lives.

This book is *not* a call to evangelical political action. Rather, it is a summons to personal renewal—a challenge to live out our faith in a way that matches words with actions. We will impact society only to the extent we allow God to impact us first. Each chapter concludes with an opportunity for you to reflect on what you've read and to respond.

So grab your passport, pack your suitcase, and come with me to visit some of the most fascinating people who inhabit the pages of the Bible! But before you begin, pause and ask God to give you an understanding mind . . . and a sensitive heart. My prayer for you matches that of Paul for his friends in the church at Ephesus. "I keep asking that the God of our Lord Jesus Christ, the glorious Father, may give you the Spirit of wisdom and revelation, so that you may know him better" (Ephesians 1:17).

IT'S DISCOURAGING TO THINK HOW
MANY PEOPLE ARE SHOCKED BY
HONESTY AND HOW FEW BY DECEIT.

—*Noel Coward*

1

UNDER THE LAMPLIGHT:
Honesty

ravel back through time over 2,300 years to Athens in the fourth century BC. As you wind through the stone streets of the city, the bright light of the sun casts harsh shadows on the stone pathway before you. You wind through these mottled streets on your way from the marketplace to your home . . . carrying your meager purchases for tonight's meal in a small sack by your side.

As you round a corner, you spot a man in the distance carrying a lighted lamp. How odd! Why is he carrying a lamp when the sun is so bright? You watch as he pushes the lamp into the faces of oncoming pedestrians. He draws closer, and now you make out the simple garb and bare feet of this walking lamppost. He is almost beside you before his shaking hands thrust the clay lamp into your face. Then he asks his penetrating question: "Are *you* an honest person?"

You've just met Diogenes . . . the Greek philosopher asking uncomfortable questions. Diogenes belonged to a school of philosophy whose members believed virtue was the only good. They sought the essence of good in self-control and independence, so while looking for an honest individual Diogenes searched for someone who was not motivated by self-interest.

You feel strangely uncomfortable by his penetrating eyes and abrupt question. What does he know about you? You hesitate but a moment before answering, but even as you begin to speak you are sure he noticed the catch in your voice. He moves on in his search for someone honest, and you head home—pondering the uncertainty of your answer.

A WHO'S WHO AMONG THE DISHONEST

If you were to ask your friends and colleagues what groups of people they felt were most untrustworthy, you might hear journalists, celebrities, telemarketers, used car salesmen, policemen, and others. But almost everyone would include politicians on such a list, and have done so for a long time. Mark Twain penned, "It could probably be shown by facts and figures that there is no distinctively native American criminal class except Congress."[6] Will Rogers wisecracked, "A politician is just like a pickpocket; it's almost impossible to get one to reform."[7] Even the French general and politician Charles de Gaulle said, "Since a politician never believes what he says, he is quite surprised to be taken at his word."[8]

We distrust politicians because some (thankfully, not all!) make outrageous promises to get elected that they cannot possibly keep. Working in Chicago has given me new insight into the reality of politics and corruption. One recent example is that of former Illinois governor Rod Blagojevich who seems to embody the hubris and deceit we have come to expect in politicians. After the governor spoke at his impeachment trial, State Senator Matt Murphy summed up the sentiment of many. "He reminded us today in real detail that he is an unusually good liar." The Senate then voted 59–0 to remove Blagojevich from office.

Unfortunately, Rod Blagojevich is not an isolated case. Three of Illinois' last seven governors have gone to prison. Amanda Paulson wrote an incisive article explaining why a "culture of corruption" seems to pervade Illinois politics. "Politicians blame, in part, Illinois' loose system of ethics and campaign-finance laws. But the deeper issue may be an entrenched political culture in which trading favors—and money—is often expected and encouraged, people enter politics thinking more about power and personal gain than public service, and the public holds their elected officials to a low standard of ethics."[9]

Diogenes would have a tough time searching out a totally

honest individual in Springfield, Illinois . . . or in Washington, D.C. Politicians are not any more evil or corrupt than society as a whole. But they are under more scrutiny because the promises they make are public. We entrust our leaders with the authority to do what is right, but they face added temptations that come with being part of the power structure. Edmund Burke wrote, "The greater the power, the more dangerous the abuse" . . . and that is a danger faced by all politicians.

An Honest Politician

Had Diogenes lived two centuries earlier, he could have found his honest man. And that honest man was a career politician! His name at birth was Daniel, which means "God is my judge." Daniel was born into a royal family in the kingdom of Judah. But his silver spoon soon tarnished. As a young man he watched the army of Nebuchadnezzar march on Jerusalem. The city surrendered, and Nebuchadnezzar demanded the collection of several royal "hostages" that he could take back to Babylon to guarantee the cooperation of this captured nation. Daniel was one of these.

Daniel spent three years in Babylon learning the language, laws, and literature of the Babylonians. He graduated *summa cum laude* . . . top honors in his class! He then entered his career in government. A career that lasted over six decades. A career that saw numerous promotions and honors. A career that spanned the rule of at least four kings in two separate empires.

In six decades a politician can make many friends—and even more enemies. Enemies seething with jealousy, envy, anger, and resentment . . . emotions that gnaw at the insides of otherwise competent people and force them into irrational acts.

The crisis came near the end of Daniel's governmental

career. The king appointed Daniel as one of the top three administrators over the government. (He had reached the level of senior cabinet minister.) But future promotions were on the horizon. "Now Daniel so distinguished himself among the administrators and the satraps by his exceptional qualities that the king planned to set him over the whole kingdom" (Daniel 6:3). Though in his eighties by this time, Daniel was still leaving the competition in the dust!

And how did his political rivals react?

"At this, the administrators and the satraps tried to find grounds for charges against Daniel in his conduct of government affairs" (Daniel 6:4a). How do you stop a politician in his tracks? Look for the dirt. Find the skeletons in the closet.

Consider how well you would fare if a group of powerful individuals secretly decided to investigate you. They would spy on you at work. Record the time you arrive each morning and the time you leave every night. Count the paper clips and pens in your drawer to see if even one is missing. Follow you home to see where you stop along the way. Look through your mail and magazines to see what you are reading. Rifle through your trash to see what you are eating. Monitor your television and your computer to see what you are watching. Check your tax returns for "irregularities" or unreported income. Look through your bank records to verify all deposits and checks. In short, what would your file look like if a group of enemies pulled out all the stops and spared no expense to uncover the "real" you?

> DANIEL HAD FAITH-FULLY DONE THOSE THINGS HE WAS ASKED TO DO TO THE BEST OF HIS ABILITY.

Picture the scene in the darkened boardroom the night the private eyes presented their report. A few flickering torches mounted on the glazed-brick walls reveal images of lions, their bared fangs and wild eyes mirroring the ferocity of the gathering band of conspirators. Packed into the room were 120 satraps and the other two administrators. They came in vengeful glee hoping to unmask Daniel and prove to themselves—and to the king—that Daniel was no better than anyone else. The investigation had been long and arduous, made even more so by the need for secrecy. Neither Daniel nor the king could know of this "private" investigation. Had Daniel known, he might have been able to block the effort or take extra precautions to hide any incriminating evidence. Had the king known, he might have shown his displeasure at their petty jealousy by ordering their dismissal . . . or their death!

The room grew silent as the chief investigator stepped to the podium. With a grim frown on his face he announced to those gathered that the investigators "could find no corruption in him, because he was trustworthy and neither corrupt nor negligent" (Daniel 6:4b). Daniel was squeaky clean!

The group of would-be antagonists reluctantly admitted two essential facts about Daniel's actions. First, they could find no evidence of corruption. Daniel had not taken bribes, skimmed money from the public treasury for private gain, received kickbacks, or provided political favors to friends. No sins of *commission* could be found.

Second, they could find no evidence of neglect. Daniel had not slacked off, cut corners, or ignored his responsibilities. He had faithfully done those things he was asked to do to the best of his ability. No sins of *omission* could be found.

No corruption. No neglect. Daniel was as honest as politicians come, and those gathered at this secret meeting had to be thinking the same thing that had been going through the king's mind: Daniel was in a league of his own.

A sharp tapping on the podium momentarily silenced the murmuring of the satraps. "Don't abandon all hope," the speaker said as his face twisted into a sinister grin. "Our search uncovered one other item." Though ignored at first, this one characteristic offered a ray of hope in an otherwise gloomy report. "We will never find any basis for charges against this man Daniel unless it has something to do with the law of his God" (Daniel 6:5).

Could there be a connection between Daniel's faith and his actions? Was Daniel such a "straight arrow" because of the heavenly Archer he served? To this group of disgruntled advisors Daniel's one vulnerability was his unswerving devotion to his God. Daniel's was so honest and consistent in his actions that an attack against his religious beliefs would not force him to change his routine.

Their plot was ingenious. Flatter the king by suggesting that all prayers for thirty days be directed only to him. Obviously the law was impractical and unenforceable, but that didn't matter. These leaders designed the law to entrap just one individual, and it worked to perfection. Daniel, Mr. Honest-as-they-come, was not about to deny his God . . . or hide his public commitment to his God. As soon as the king signed the law, the conspirators hurried to Daniel's house. Some gathered in the street along the west side of Daniel's house, others climbed to the roof of the building just across the street. They were all seeking a clear view into one particular window in Daniel's house—an upstairs window that opened toward the west, toward Jerusalem! For nearly seventy years Daniel had lived in Babylon, but he never forgot his hometown, or his faith. This was the place where he had prayed daily, and they were hoping he wouldn't stop now. As they expected, they found him praying in his open window "just as he had done before" (Daniel 6:10).

Anyone can display godly character when the going is easy. Few steal if they are satisfied with what they possess. Few lie when speaking the truth is to their advantage. Few cheat on exams when they know all the answers. But character is formed in the crucible of adversity.

The key to Daniel's success in surviving both the political investigation and the infamous lions' den that followed was his honesty. After his miraculous deliverance Daniel explained why he had been spared. "My God sent his angel, and he shut the mouths of the lions. They have not hurt me, because I was found innocent in his sight. Nor have I ever done any wrong before you, O king" (Daniel 6:22).

Where Has Honesty Gone?

Honesty is a character trait held in high regard throughout history. Millions of American schoolchildren grew up knowing the tale of George Washington confessing to his father, "I cannot tell a lie. I chopped down the cherry tree." Now, it is a bit disconcerting to find out the story is untrue! Mason Weems, an American Episcopal clergyman, who wrote a popular biography of George Washington entitled *The Life and Memorable Actions of George Washington*, invented the story. Somehow it seems ironic that a clergyman falsified a story about George Washington because he wanted to teach children about honesty.

Though the story was not true, the lesson conveyed did influence another American some years later. Abraham Lincoln was born in Kentucky and grew up on the Indiana frontier. Formal education was the exception on the edge of civilization, but two books profoundly influenced Lincoln's life. The first was the Bible, and the second was Mason Weems's biography of George Washington. With these two books as his guide, is it any wonder that Abraham Lincoln became known as "Honest Abe"?

In just over a century the Western world has moved from extolling the virtue of honesty to believing that honesty is not always the best policy. Don't get me wrong. I'm *not* saying that society was honest a century ago. Dishonesty has marred God's creation almost from the beginning. The first tempter, Satan, is called "a liar" (John 8:44). But the frequency of lying and the acceptability of lying has increased at an alarming rate.

Sadly, this trend is as true for those who claim to follow Christ as it is for those who don't. Rod Handley highlighted the severity of the problem. "Numerous studies indicate that Christians are just as likely as non-Christians to falsify tax returns, plagiarize, bribe, shift blame, ignore construction specifications, illegally copy software, steal from the workplace, and selectively obey the laws of the land."[10]

Trust is a fragile commodity. Once lost, it is extremely difficult to recover. We struggle to trust someone caught in a lie.

Why Bother with Honesty?

In the back of our minds we all believe in the virtue of honesty. And yet, we all struggle with being honest. Well, actually we don't like to think of it in those terms. We prefer to say we "fudge" a little on a report or test. We only tell "little white lies" so we won't hurt the feelings of others. And we "shade the truth" to enhance our popularity or fit in with the crowd. In effect, we lie to ourselves about our dishonesty with others.

But why should we tell the truth? What personal benefits will honesty bring? The Bible presents three specific, positive results of honesty. Honesty promotes trust, provides a positive role model for others, and pleases God.

Honesty promotes trust

Whom do you trust? Stop right now and make a list of five individuals you consider to be trustworthy. They may be close friends, church or community leaders, coworkers, radio or television personalities, national or international leaders. But the one common element must be that you trust them. Now look at your list and ask yourself what elements these individuals have in common. One specific item I'm sure they share is that you perceive them to be people who are honest. What they say, what they do with their money, how they perform at work, how they treat others—you trust those who have a reputation for honesty in these areas.

> IF YOU LIE TO OTHERS, NO MATTER HOW SMALL OR INSIGNIFICANT THE LIE IS, EVENTUALLY YOU WILL BE EXPOSED.

Now, make a list of five individuals you don't trust. They can be people you know or public figures. Again, look at the list and ask yourself what elements these individuals share. Those you trust least are those you perceive to be dishonest. They have lied, cheated, or been dishonest in some way . . . and that's why you don't trust them.

Why is God trustworthy? Because He doesn't lie and He doesn't make empty promises. In short, He's honest. Period. We stake our eternal destiny on God's promises. "We accept man's testimony, but God's testimony is greater because it is the testimony of God . . . And this is the testimony: God has given us eternal life, and this life is in his Son. He who has the Son has life; he who does not have the Son of God does not have life" (1 John 5:9, 11–12). God's honesty to us promotes trust in Him. And that trust is essential for our eternal destiny.

Are you trustworthy? You like to think so. (You certainly *hope* others trust you!) But trust is a by-product of honesty. If you lie to others, no matter how small or insignificant the lie is, eventually you will be exposed. To the extent you compromise your standards of honesty, you will lower the level of trust others have in you.

Honesty provides a positive role model

The past few decades have seen a steep decline in honesty. People distrust politicians, and what little trust remains erodes deeper at each election when candidates hurl charges and countercharges against each other. Political commercials, blending half-truths and distorted facts, promote one candidate by tearing down the character of another. Even "Honest Abe" would have struggled under all the mud hurled by today's politicians.

Yet this is no time for Christians to give up. The truth of God's Word shines most brightly in the darkness. The age we live in does not have a monopoly on dishonesty. The same moral decline gripped the Roman Empire when the church began. Christians stood out because they displayed characteristics that were lacking in those around them.

The island of Crete epitomized the cesspool of moral values in the Roman world. In Greek literature "to Cretanize" was a euphemism for lying. In Titus 1 the apostle Paul quoted the Cretan poet Epimenides who described the moral state of his country five centuries earlier. "Cretans are always liars, evil brutes, lazy gluttons." Then Paul explained that the evaluation was still valid. "This testimony is true."

How could a society with a history of dishonesty ever change? The answer rested in the positive role models of those believers living in Crete. Paul spent the next chapter explaining how older men (2:2), older women (2:3), young women (2:4–5), young men (2:6–8), and even slaves (2:9–10) could become examples who could influence society. Titus was to "teach what is in accord with sound doctrine" (2:1). Cretans may have been known the world over as liars, but the believers in Crete were to live by a different standard.

Passing new laws won't make society honest. There are not enough police today to enforce the laws already on the books. Technology won't make society honest. The Internal Revenue Service uses sophisticated computer programs to uncover tax fraud, but many still cheat on their income tax returns. Stores spend billions of dollars on security, but shoplifting continues.

The world needs examples of honesty in action. They need role models of Christians who live out their faith in real life.

Honesty pleases God

The bottom-line question on the issue of honesty is not how we feel about the issue but how God feels. What is God's view of honesty?

In Proverbs 11:1 Solomon wrote, "The Lord abhors dishonest scales, but accurate weights are his delight." The marketplace buzzed with activity. Each vendor called to those passing by, trying to get them to stop and shop. Children laughed and darted through the crowd, prompting distracted mothers to stop haggling just long enough to shout an unheeded word of warning. The aroma of freshly baked bread mixed with the fragrance of hyssop and the pungent smell of yogurt. Baskets of grain and jars of wine sat beside piles of grapes and figs just outside the city gate. Bargaining was brisk as the vendors hawked their wares. After agreeing on the price, the vendor would set up a pair of scales. The seller would place the appropriate weights on one side while the buyer placed some silver on the other. When the scales balanced, the payment was sufficient.

No bureaucracy existed to test and certify the scales of

that day. Archaeologists have discovered stone weights at numerous sites, and no two sets of weights match exactly. The temptation for the seller was great to make each weight just a fraction heavier than the accepted standard. The average buyer would never know he or she had paid just slightly more than necessary during the transaction. But God knew. The point of Solomon's proverb is that *God* is the one who is pleased, or displeased, by such actions.

God expects honesty from those who claim Him as their heavenly Father. He wants His children to share His "family likeness" . . . and that includes honesty. Yet some Christians use honesty as an excuse for being rude and obnoxious. Does being honest mean we must be offensive?

SPEAK THE TRUTH . . . AND IN LOVE

In writing to the Ephesians, the apostle Paul spent the first half of his letter describing the spiritual wealth God had bestowed on His church. In the second half of the letter Paul focused on the "so what" of each believer's new position. A believer's new position in Christ should bring practical changes in his or her day-to-day conduct. One of the first areas of change named by Paul is in the area of honesty. "Therefore each of you must put off falsehood and speak truthfully to his neighbor, for we are all members of one body" (Ephesians 4:25).

But we must view Paul's command within the larger context. Just a few verses earlier Paul focused on the motive that is to guide all speech. "Instead, speaking the truth *in love*, we will in all things grow up into him who is the Head" (Ephesians 4:15, italics added). Some things may be truthful, but they are best left unsaid if the one speaking is not motivated by love.

Honesty—guided by love—is always the best policy. Sometimes love requires us to hold our tongue rather than lashing back in an unkind way. But at other times love requires us to tell a friend what they need to hear, even if the words are not what they want to hear. Such honesty will deepen most true friendships.

Solomon spoke of a friend's honesty in the book of Proverbs. True friends are those we trust to say the hard things . . . the rebukes that reveal blind spots in our lives. Solomon described the value of such honesty from friends.

Proverbs 27:6 "Wounds from a friend can be trusted, but an enemy multiplies kisses."
[A friend tells you what you need to hear, even if the truth hurts.]

Proverbs 27:9 "Perfume and incense bring joy to the heart, and the pleasantness of one's friend springs from his earnest counsel."
[Honest advice from a friend should make us thankful for his or her counsel.]

Proverbs 27:17 "As iron sharpens iron, so one man sharpens another."
[A true friend sometimes causes "friction and sparks" in our life, but the results are always positive.]

Reflect and Respond

Honesty isn't always easy. It can be uncomfortable, embarrassing, and unpopular . . . but God expects His children to share His passion for honesty.

1. In what areas of your life do you struggle with complete honesty?
2. What can you do in the next seven days to become more honest in your words and deeds?
3. Do you recall any specific instances in your past where your dishonesty hurt others? Pray and ask God to help you resolve the matter, even if it requires confession and restitution.
4. Memorize Ephesians 4:15 and consciously try to "speak the truth in love" in the coming days.

"Listen, for I have worthy things to say; I open my lips to speak what is right. My mouth speaks what is true, for my lips detest wickedness." (Proverbs 8:6–7)

COMPASSION IS SOMETIMES THE FATAL
CAPACITY FOR FEELING WHAT IT IS LIKE
TO LIVE INSIDE SOMEBODY ELSE'S SKIN.
IT IS THE KNOWLEDGE THAT THERE CAN
NEVER REALLY BE ANY PEACE AND JOY
FOR ME UNTIL THERE IS PEACE AND JOY
FINALLY FOR YOU TOO.

—*Frederick Buechner*

2

WIDOWS AND WHEATFIELDS:
Compassion

IS COMPASSION OUT OF FASHION?

Warning! Too much compassion may be hazardous to your health! That could have been the title of a humorous article that appeared in the *Dallas Morning News*. The writer described the almost disastrous efforts of a kind librarian to help a stranded motorist:

> She was driving along and saw this man, standing beside his car, trying to flag somebody down. She stopped and he said the battery was dead and asked if she'd mind giving him a shove to start his car.
>
> "Why, certainly," she said, "but I've never done this before."
>
> "Well, just get your speed up to about 30, shove me along for a short distance and that should start it."
>
> "Are you sure?"
>
> "Certainly, I've done it a hundred times."
>
> She backed up her car. Backed it up some more. And some more. Then she gunned the motor, burned rubber and came barreling like a missile toward the back of the man's car. He turned white as a ghost, screamed, prayed, jumped to the side of his car and started madly waving his arms. "No! Nooooo! Stop! Stoooopppp!" She mashed hard on the brakes, skidded and managed to avoid a total disaster. "He did not," she said, "ever tell me I was supposed to put my bumper up against his first."[11]

We chuckle at this story because it reminds us of situations in our lives where a lack of understanding caused problems. But the story has one sad twist. Most of us cannot fully relate to the librarian because we would *never* stop along the highway to help a stranger. Our fear of being robbed—or worse!—keeps us in our cars with our windows up and our doors locked. Compassion takes a back seat to fear.

But fear is not the fiercest foe of compassion. Selfishness is. The natural tendency is to "look out for ol' number one—myself." We do not care for others because we are more absorbed with ourselves.

THE NATION'S "TERRIBLE TWOS"

The United States has barely passed through the celebration of its second century as a nation. Just out of diapers historically, it's a mere youngster among some other world civilizations. If the United States were an actual child, perhaps we could attribute its present selfishness and violence to "the terrible twos"—that age when a formerly sweet child becomes defiant.

The Bible presents a detailed account of another nation that struggled through its "terrible twos." The nation was Israel. Just two centuries after entering God's Promised Land, Israel was out of control. Like the "terrible two" it was, the nation stamped its feet and said no to God. Childish tantrums, foolish actions, and violent outbursts alternated with periods of relative peace and calm. A strong, active parent can help modify these childish outbursts, but that leader was absent in Israel. It was the time of the judges when "Israel had no king; everyone did as he saw fit" (Judges 17:6; 18:1; 19:1; 21:25).

A two-year-old without parental observation is a frightening thought. Picture your home being invaded by a curious, unsupervised toddler. The potential for material damage or physical harm is immense! The child needs supervision.

But how does a selfish nation produce a compassionate king? Where could Israel turn to find the kind of leader it needed in its time of desperation? God revealed the answer in the book of Ruth.

FROM BARRENNESS TO BLESSING

The historical background to the events recorded in the book of Ruth is given in 1:1—"in the days when the judges ruled." This was a period of national, religious, and moral decay when foreign powers oppressed the people of Israel. The difficulties experienced by the nation during the period of the judges resulted from their disobedience to God's law. From Moab and Midian in the east (Judges 3:12–14; 6:1), to the king of Hazor in the north (4:1–3), to the Philistines in the west (13:1), Israel chafed under the yoke of foreign oppression. Hordes of men on camels swarmed through the Jezreel Valley (6:3–5), and individuals had to harvest in secret to keep from having their meager resources looted (6:11). Life in the times of the judges was harsh.

The individual story of God's provision for Naomi through the faithfulness of Boaz and Ruth parallels the national story of God's provision for the nation through the descendant of Boaz and Ruth.

Naomi, her husband, and their two children crossed from Israel to Moab to pursue a better life. Refugees fleeing famine, they hoped to start over in this new country. Excitement turned to grief, however, when Naomi's husband died. Naomi, now a middle-aged woman with two older sons, saw her options dwindle. The marriages of the sons to "foreign" women caused a twinge of guilt, but the daughters-in-law proved to be wonderful wives who displayed great love for their husbands and their new mother-in-law.

Tragedy struck less than ten years later when both sons died unexpectedly Three grieving widows sat together lamenting their unbearable misfortune when word arrived that the famine in Israel had ended. A bitter, barren Naomi summoned the last of her resolve and decided it was time to return home.

Her faithful daughters-in-law obediently packed their belongings to join Naomi on her journey. Naomi released them from their obligation and urged them to return to their families. Weeping, Orpah turned back, but the other refused to go. "Where you go I will go, and where you stay I will stay. Your people will be my people and your God my God" (Ruth 1:16). Ruth cared for Naomi, and her compassion came from the truth she had learned about Naomi's God.

The journey from Moab to Bethlehem was brutal. They first had to cross the Dead Sea, doing so at the tongue of land jutting out near the southern end. They then hiked north to En Gedi where a narrow pathway snaked its way up the steep cliffs and into the rugged Judean Wilder-

> IT'S NATURAL FOR TENSIONS TO EXIST BETWEEN OWNERS AND WORKERS, BETWEEN THE HAVES AND THE HAVE-NOTS.

ness. The entire journey was sixty miles—four days of hard walking, down and up thousands of feet in elevation, carrying everything (including water)! The long trek brought the exhausted women through the twisted landscape of the Dead Sea and Judean Wilderness. Finally the two women walked wearily into Bethlehem. Realistically, the situation looked grim for Naomi and Ruth. Both were widows without husbands to protect and provide for them. They had no wealth, no resources, no prospects. The younger woman was a stranger who would face the stigma and prejudice of being a "foreigner." No strong government existed to care for them. This was the time of the judges, remember. If two individuals ever needed compassion, Naomi and Ruth were the ones.

Along Comes Boaz

Striding across the opening verse of Ruth 2 is Boaz. Besides introducing him as a relative of Naomi's former husband, the writer also pictures him as "a man of standing" (2:1). In most Western countries today we associate that phrase with wealth, power, prestige, leadership. And all of these are involved to some extent. Boaz does have enough wealth to control numerous fields, and he maintains control over those who work for him. But the phrase also hints at Boaz's moral condition. He has a good reputation among the people. He is a man of integrity and character. He is a man of compassion. And this side of his personality plays a key role in the remainder of the story. Boaz displays four characteristics of compassion that made him a man of standing in Bethlehem.

He spoke kindly

Driven by a need to gather food for her mother-in-law and herself, Ruth made her way out to the fields of golden barley that surrounded Bethlehem like a patchwork quilt. God's Law allowed her to follow the workers and pick up those pieces of grain they dropped. God had specifically told the Israelites, "When you reap the harvest of your land, do not reap to the very edges of your field or gather the gleanings of your harvest. Leave them for the poor and the alien" (Leviticus 23:22). Ruth, both poor and alien, certainly qualified for this provision!

Boaz visited his fields to supervise the harvest and observe the progress of his laborers. A social chasm separated Boaz from his laborers. He was the man of standing, they were the hired servants. He owned the fields, they worked in them. It's natural for tensions to exist between owners and workers, between the haves and the have-nots. But Boaz didn't look down on his servants.

As Boaz arrived at the fields being harvested, he greeted the harvesters. "The Lord be with you!" They responded in kind. "The Lord bless you!" Boaz's words reveal his kind spirit. He cared for his workers, and he was verbal in expressing his greeting and love. The workers' response hints of their appreciation for him. Boaz was a kind employer, and they respected him.

He cared deeply

Words are an important way to express compassion, but words ring hollow if they are not accompanied by actions. Boaz could speak kindly because he was kindhearted. His care blazed most brightly when he spotted Ruth gleaning among his workers. When Boaz asked the foreman about Ruth, the foreman gave a succinct answer (Ruth 2:6–7).

- "She is the Moabitess" (she's a foreigner)
- "who came back from Moab with Naomi."
  (she's faithful to her mother-in-law)
- "She said, 'Please let me glean and gather'."
  (she's respectful of authority)
- "She . . . has worked steadily from morning till now."
  (she's a hard worker)

Boaz showed his care by providing for Ruth's protection and provision. A single woman, especially a foreigner, faced danger when she ventured alone into the fields. Boaz encouraged Ruth to stay with his reapers. "I have told the men not to touch you" (Ruth 2:9). He also went out of his way to provide for her physical needs. "And whenever you are thirsty, go and get a drink from the water jars the men have filled." Boaz followed his words of kindness with specific actions.

He accepted warmly

Some might think Boaz was attracted to Ruth only because of her beauty, but the text suggests otherwise. Boaz was first impressed by her faithfulness and devotion to her mother-in-law and by her hard work. After his kind protection Ruth bowed in amazement and asked, "Why have I found such favor in your eyes that you notice me—a foreigner?" (Ruth 2:10). Ruth realized that not all Israelites appreciated her presence. Though she had been in town only a short time, she may already have heard the verbal slurs and seen the little signs of hostility that said, "You're not one of us!" Why was Boaz so different?

Boaz's answer spoke volumes. "I've been told all about what you have done for your mother-in-law" (Ruth 2:11). When Boaz looked at Ruth he did not see a Moabitess. Instead, he saw a daughter-in-law who cared so deeply for her mother-in-law she was willing to risk racial slurs and personal attacks to provide the food her mother-in-law needed.

Boaz saw Ruth through the eyes of God. And he wished for God's blessing to be on this kindhearted foreigner. "May the Lord repay you for what you have done. May you be richly rewarded by the Lord, the God of Israel, under whose wings you have come to take refuge" (Ruth 2:12).

Some in Bethlehem may have barely tolerated the presence of this foreigner in their midst. Perhaps they resented her because of earlier battles between Moab and Israel. Certainly many Israelites lost their lives when Eglon king of Moab oppressed Israel for eighteen years (Judges 3:12–14). Perhaps they begrudged her the pieces of grain she took from the fields—grain they may have coveted for themselves. But Boaz was different. He saw her faithfulness and hoped the Lord would bless her. Little did he know God would answer his wish . . . through him!

Ruth was appreciative. Though her social standing was lower than "one of your servant girls," Boaz displayed acceptance. That Boaz had "given [her] comfort" and "spoken kindly" (Ruth 2:13)—two basic acts of compassion often in short supply—overwhelmed Ruth.

He acted generously

Boaz had kind intentions, but his compassion was also practical. Words of comfort are nothing more than idle wishes unless they are accompanied by generous deeds. We have all known individuals who "know all the right words" but who never move their intentions from their mouth to their hands.

At midday the heat in Bethlehem was most oppressive. The sun shown directly overhead from a cloudless sky, its intensity sapping the strength of those who had been at work since sunup. The workers drifted to the protection of the temporary booths set up beside the fields. Here, clay pots held water while freshly roasted grain and bread provided nourishment for the weary workers. Sprawling on the ground, the workers rested and shared the latest news and gossip. The shade was refreshing, the water was cool, and the bread freshly baked. The hired laborers expected such arrangements, but the owner had no obligation to provide for those who were not in his employment.

> RUTH FOUND PROTECTION, ACCEPTANCE, AND ENCOURAGEMENT. IN SHORT, SHE FOUND COMPASSION.

Ruth had no illusions of receiving special favors the morning she first went to the harvest fields. Her greatest hope would be that no one would harass her. Boaz's earlier words of kindness had taken her by surprise, but at noon he approached her and said, "Come over here. Have some bread and dip it in the wine vinegar." As Ruth stepped into the shade of the booth with the other workers, "he offered her some roasted grain" (Ruth 2:14). Boaz's generosity must have amazed Ruth. "She ate all she wanted and had some left over." Boaz was not stingy with his words of praise . . . or his food!

Boaz met Ruth's immediate needs for food, rest, and shelter. But his generosity extended beyond those specific acts of visible kindness. As she left, he turned to his men and ordered them to be inefficient harvesters for Ruth's sake! "Even if she gathers among the sheaves, don't embarrass her. Rather, pull out some stalks for her from the bundles and leave them for her to pick up, and don't rebuke her" (2:15–16). Boaz provided for Ruth's long-term needs, and he did so in a way that protected her dignity.

After just one day, Naomi knew God was at work. When Ruth returned from the harvest, she carried over half a bushel of grain. That was far more than one would expect for a single worker picking up stray pieces of grain that had fallen from the harvesters' hands. No wonder Naomi asked, "Where did you glean today? Where did you work? Blessed be the man who took notice of you!" (Ruth 2:19).

Boaz's generosity extended throughout the barley and wheat harvests. For nearly two months Ruth worked alongside Boaz's laborers. She found protection, acceptance, and encouragement. In short, she found compassion.

THE RESULTS OF COMPASSION

One man's compassion made the difference in the lives of two widowed women—Ruth and Naomi. The story provides a bright spot in an otherwise dark chapter in Israel's history. While everyone else was "doing what was right in their own eyes," Boaz did what was right in God's eyes. But what difference could such acts of kindness make nationally? Could the compassion of one man in one small town influence the entire nation? The final chapter of the book of Ruth says yes!

As in a charming fairy tale, Ruth and Boaz overcame adversity and got married. But instead of picturing the couple living "happily ever after," the writer ends by sharing the legacy the couple left that extended far beyond their days in Israel. Ruth and Boaz had a son named Obed. That child grew up and had a son named Jesse. He grew up and had eight sons—the youngest of whom became King David! The compassion of Ruth for Naomi and the compassion of Boaz for Ruth ultimately produced Israel's greatest king. The book that begins "in the days when the judges ruled" (1:1) ends with David, the king who set the nation aright. The pivotal link in the transition from chaos to kingdom in the book of Ruth was the compassion of Ruth and Boaz!

Hesed Projects

I first started teaching in 1981. In those earlier years of my teaching I was far more "academic" in my approach. I had midterm and final exams because I wanted my students to memorize key Bible facts. But one summer my perspective changed completely.

I was teaching my favorite class, a survey of the prophets, in a five-week summer session. I had midterm and final exams already prepared. Everything was ready, and I was excited (perhaps even a bit proud). My students would come away understanding each of the Old Testament prophets.

But something went radically wrong that summer. Over the five-week period I taught my course, three individuals whom I had known while a student at seminary failed morally. Each destroyed his family, damaged a ministry, and brought disrespect to the name of Christ. But how could it happen? We had sat through the same seminary classes, studied the same Bible, taken the same tests. Yet the truth of God's Word had somehow not penetrated their hearts. Something was wrong!

That traumatic summer changed my approach to teaching. As I prayed through what I could do to help other students avoid those pitfalls, I concluded that merely memorizing facts was not enough. We can become hardened to God's Word unless we work to apply it to our lives. We can grow cold in our relationships with others unless we work hard to cultivate compassion, concern, and care.

I replaced my midterm and final exams with "*hesed* projects," and I still tell my students these are the most important projects they will have to do all year. They must complete two such projects to pass any course I teach. But what is a "*hesed* project"? Let me quote from my class syllabus.

Hesed is the Old Testament word for "loyalty love" that has the implied idea of loving faithfulness to a covenant relationship. The Old Testament wisdom literature and prophets continually stress the need for covenant faithfulness—both to God and to man. One danger in school is the tendency to become "hearers of the Word only"— to divorce knowledge from response. Believers must take time to cultivate and maintain covenant faithfulness in their relationships with others. These two *hesed* projects are given in place of midterm and final exams to give each student an opportunity to find time to develop "loyalty love" with others.

Each "project" includes the following elements.

1. Plan an activity that you and someone else can do that will:
   • last about four hours

- not involve school
- be a time of Christian fellowship and enjoyment.
2. Participate in the activity.
3. Write a summary and turn it in on the midterm and final reports.

I encourage the students to be creative in planning projects. If they are married, they might want to go on a picnic, go to the zoo, go biking with their family, or visit some other place they have never seen. For those who are married the emphasis is on doing something the whole family can enjoy. If they are single, I tell them to take a friend to dinner, go on a hike together, go fishing, or go to a sporting event. They are to take time to enjoy the fellowship of another's company.

The response has been overwhelming. I have a file of cards, letters, and hand-drawn pictures from the spouses and children of students thanking me for the *hesed* project assignment. I receive calls from former students who tell me they still have family *hesed* projects.

Loyalty love and compassion fit together. Someone committed to a relationship will demonstrate care and compassion to the other individual. In Lamentations 3 Jeremiah found God's loyalty love and compassion to be twin pillars of hope. "Because of the Lord's great love (*hesed*) we are not consumed, for his compassions never fail" (Lamentations 3:22). How deep is *your* reservoir of compassion?

Reflect and Respond

Think of someone on the forefront of business or politics, and you usually envision someone who is hard driving, tough, aggressive. But an individual on the vanguard of the Christian life is a man or woman of compassion. Take some time to focus on several practical questions related to compassion:

1. Are there individuals you know to whom you find it difficult to show compassion? If so, why do you find it so difficult to show care and compassion for them?
2. Think of someone who has shown compassion to you—what were the circumstances?
3. Choose one individual and try to get to know that person better this week. Ask God for one specific opportunity to show compassion to that person.
4. Memorize Lamentations 3:22 and ask God to remind you of the compassion He has shown to you.
5. What other biblical characters showed compassion? How? What resulted?
6. Think of a *hesed* project and do it!

"If you have any encouragement from being united with Christ, if any comfort from his love, if any fellowship with the Spirit, if any tenderness and compassion, then make my joy complete by being like-minded, having the same love, being one in spirit and purpose." (Philippians 2:1–2)

THE BIGGEST DIFFICULTY WITH MANKIND
TODAY IS THAT OUR KNOWLEDGE HAS
INCREASED SO MUCH FASTER THAN OUR
WISDOM.

—*Frank Whitmore*

3

THE PHOTO
ALBUM:
Wisdom

KNOWLEDGE OR WISDOM?

All right, I confess. I like offbeat comics. My wife tolerates my passion for the oddball. I read *Dilbert*, *Pearls before Swine*, and *Zits* regularly. I also have the book collections of past *Calvin and Hobbes* and *Far Side* comics. In fact, I struggled with withdrawal symptoms when Gary Larson stopped producing *Far Side* and when Bill Watterson stopped drawing *Calvin and Hobbes*. Much truth can be found in humor.

One of my favorite *Far Side* cartoons of all time shows outside steps leading up to Midvale School for the Gifted. At the top of the steps stands one of these gifted students, books cradled in his right hand, with his left hand vainly pushing against the outside door to open it. Just above the student is a sign on the door that says (in very *large* letters) "PULL." All right, don't laugh. But you would . . . if you saw the picture.

That particular comic speaks to me because it distinguishes between knowledge and wisdom. The students attending the school in Larson's comic strip were expected to have a high level of knowledge. That doesn't guarantee they are wise.

The Internet has made the twenty-first century the "information age." Instant access to unlimited information promises to usher in the technological millennium for humanity. The assumption seems to be that availability of information will lead to greater wisdom and understanding.

But you cannot equate information with wisdom. There is a large chasm between accessing data and acquiring wisdom. Data and information (not all of it accurate) abound online. But most individuals still make poor choices in how they live their lives.

The Hebrews understood the difference between knowledge and wisdom. Their word for wisdom (*hokmah*) carried with it the idea of skill. Wisdom was the ability to live life skillfully and successfully. Knowledge alone doesn't guarantee that life will be lived skillfully.

Society is awash in a sea of information—but people can still make very foolish choices. We know the harmful effects of smoking, excessive drinking, and drugs; but all three still entice and enslave otherwise intelligent people.

When some small problem threatens to undo an otherwise good thing, we describe it as "the fly in the ointment." The phrase originally came from the pen of the wisest of Israel's kings—Solomon. He had a knack for "turning a phrase," and the whole proverb went, "As dead flies give perfume a bad smell, so a little folly outweighs wisdom and honor" (Ecclesiastes 10:1). The phrase teaches us much about wisdom and folly—and about Solomon. To understand the full meaning of Solomon's words we need to sit down, take out the family album, and study three snapshots of Solomon taken at different times in his life.

SNAPSHOT #1:
YOUNG SOLOMON IS ASKING FOR WISDOM

"King David is dead! Long live King Solomon!" The words swirled through Jerusalem's dusty streets and echoed off the stone walls of this fortress-city. David lived his life in epic proportions, both in his triumphs and in his tragedies. The shadow of Israel's greatest warrior and king threatened to obscure his young heir to the throne. Following a legend is tough.

David's unwise marriages to multiple wives compounded by his adultery with Bathsheba produced a chaotic and fractured home. One son raped his half sister and was, in turn, murdered by his half brother (2 Samuel 13). One son led a civil war against King David and received support from

Bathsheba's grandfather (2 Samuel 15). At the end of David's life one son plotted to succeed him as king, only to be thwarted when David appointed Solomon (1 Kings 1). Had they lived back then, Oprah, Dr. Phil, and Jerry Springer would have clamored to put David's family on their shows!

Now young Solomon sits uneasily on his father's throne. His father's last words of advice were whispered warnings about Joab, David's former military commander who had plotted to make Solomon's brother king. Solomon's first act as king (after another plot to usurp his throne) was to give orders to execute the two conspirators—his own half brother and Joab (1 Kings 2). What had he gotten himself into!?!

The burden of following in the footsteps of his illustrious father, reigning wisely as king, and knowing how to discern between right and wrong gnawed at the young king. Anyone ever thrust into a place of leadership and responsibility knows the sense of inadequacy that must have gripped Solomon. He was now responsible for making life-and-death decisions. Things that seemed so clear to him as he stood on the periphery now seemed complex and involved as he tried to explore all sides to make fair and impartial judgments.

Two dangers face an individual thrust into a position of power and authority. One danger is that the leader will become paralyzed by the enormity of the task. The leader is responsible for others, and a single mistake or miscalculation can cost those followers their jobs, their families, or their lives.

Most decisions are not black-and-white. The leader must sort through conflicting reports, incomplete data, and divided supporters to decide what is best. A leader can become so afraid of making a mistake that he or she will analyze—and reanalyze—every possible angle and option . . . and do nothing unless one option emerges as the clear choice. Some call this paralysis by analysis.

The second danger is that the leader will become self-centered and prideful. Position brings with it prestige and perks, and a leader can become sidetracked by these trappings of power. Most corrupt politicians do not enter politics with evil motives. They begin with a genuine desire to make a difference. But the constant pressures and demands of those who seek their attention and help gradually desensitize them. A leader can then justify receiving gifts from those seeking access, accepting financial rewards for political favors, or even taking kickbacks from those who receive government contracts.

Alone. Vulnerable. Uncertain. Unsure how to proceed. Solomon must have doubted his father's wisdom in making him king. He was *not* the warrior his father had been. But he had inherited his father's desire to follow God. And so it's no surprise that our first snapshot of Solomon finds him kneeling before God and asking for wisdom.

Solomon traveled nearly eight miles northwest from Jerusalem to Gibeon to seek the Lord because God's temple in Jerusalem was still nothing more than a dream passed on from David to his son. Four more years would pass before Solomon could begin the temple project.

So Solomon traveled to Gibeon "for that was the most important high place" (1 Kings 3:4). What made it so important? "The tabernacle of the Lord, which Moses had made in the desert, and the altar of burnt offering were at that time on the high place at Gibeon" (1 Chronicles 21:29). Did Solomon walk or ride? We don't know, but even by foot the journey would only have taken a few hours. The procession included a thousand noisy animals to be offered as burnt offerings. The dust kicked up by the people and animals announced their presence long before the party arrived at the round, terraced hill sitting by the road leading from the hills to the Philistine plain.

Solomon made a pilgrimage to the tent of God built by Moses himself. He stood before the altar first consecrated by Moses almost five hundred years earlier and offered sacrifices to the living God. Perhaps Solomon looked for strength in his spiritual heritage. Perhaps he felt so inadequate he longed for a visible sign of God's blessing. Whatever his motivation, his willingness to offer a thousand burnt offerings on the altar demonstrated his dedication to God and his dependence on God for the task ahead.

Many leaders struggle with a crushing sense of their own inadequacy. Their followers put them on pedestals and assume they see all, hear all, know all, and can do all. But true leaders know better. They see beyond the hype and hoopla to understand their limitations and inadequacies. Solomon came to God because he was acutely aware of his need for God's help.

The Lord responded to Solomon's act of worship and devotion. Appearing to him at night, God made the ultimate offer: "Ask for whatever you want me to give you" (1 Kings 3:5). God offered Solomon the chance of a lifetime!

> **THE LORD WAITED FOR SOLOMON'S ANSWER. WHAT SHOULD HE ASK FOR? MONEY? SECURITY? PROTECTION? LONG LIFE?**

A persistent childhood fantasy is the desire to have all our wishes fulfilled. Our childhood desire to possess Aladdin's lamp might be replaced with the hope of winning the Publishers Clearing House sweepstakes—or the state lottery! Be honest: the thought of "having it all" is appealing.

What's amazing about this first snapshot of Solomon is how he responded to God's offer. Foremost in his mind was his need for wisdom, not wealth. "Now, O Lord my God, you have made your servant king in place of my father David. But I am only a little child and do not know how to carry out my duties" (1 Kings 3:7). Solomon sensed his inexperience and inadequacy.

The Lord waited for Solomon's answer. What should he ask for? Money? Security? Protection? Long life? Solomon's answer was profound in its simplicity and honesty. "So give your servant a discerning heart to govern your people and to distinguish between right and wrong. For who is able to govern this great people of yours?" (1 Kings 3:9). Solomon asked God for wisdom to do what was right in leading the people of Israel.

God rewarded Solomon for his humble request. "The Lord was pleased that Solomon had asked for this" (1 Kings 3:10). Solomon put his responsibility to Israel ahead of any desire for personal reward. God not only gave Solomon the "wise and discerning heart" he requested (3:12), God also rewarded Solomon with "riches and honor" (3:13). God promised Solomon he would be wise . . . and wealthy!

So how did Solomon do? The writer of 1 Kings includes five incidents that reveal the extent of the wisdom God gave Solomon.

Wisdom to discern truth

The first test for Solomon's God-given wisdom was not long in coming. Two prostitutes came before the king—each claiming custody of a newborn baby boy. Both women had given birth to children, but one child had died. Each woman claimed the dead child belonged to the other while she was the legitimate parent of the child who remained alive.

The child still alive was but a baby—too young to help in establishing identity. No witnesses were present to vouch for either woman. DNA testing was not available. Each story was plausible, and each woman was passionate in arguing her side. How could Solomon administer justice when the truth could not be established beyond a reasonable doubt?

Solomon revealed his God-given wisdom in his response to the women. His apparent decision to slice the living child in half and divide him between the women brought out the compassion of the true mother. Solomon then awarded the child to the rightful woman. He looked beyond the obvious to establish justice . . . and his wisdom made an impression on others. "When all Israel heard the verdict the king had given, they held the king in awe, because they saw that he had wisdom from God to administer justice" (1 Kings 3:28).

One little postscript. As a young boy I remember hearing this story in Sunday school. The finer points of the story were lost on me, but I walked home from church with a vivid picture of a king in purple robes and a crown holding a child's ankle in his left hand while raising a sword in his right to slice the boy in two. A few months later I put the story to use. Our next door neighbor had four girls. (The oldest was my age.) I was playing in my backyard when I overheard two of the younger girls arguing over a Barbie doll. Each was trying to wrest control of the doll away from the other as they shouted, "It's mine!" "No, it's mine!" Very Solomon-like I walked over, grabbed the doll, and offered to break it in half and give each sister a piece. When one screamed, "No!" I handed her the doll and told her it was hers. I felt very smug until the other sister went home to tell her mom that her sister and I were picking on her! Oh well, it worked for Solomon.

Wisdom to organize efficiently

David built Israel into a great empire, but Solomon organized it to operate smoothly. He developed an efficient central government and divided Israel into twelve districts, each with a district governor (1 Kings 4:1–19). Solomon also ruled over those surrounding nations captured by David. Evidently Solomon ruled these lands well, because the writer of Kings notes that he "had peace on all sides" (1 Kings 4:24). Solomon's organizational skills brought a time of security and prosperity unknown in the land of Israel up to that day. From "Dan to Beersheba"—from north to south in the land—the people "lived in safety, each man under his own vine and fig tree" (1 Kings 4:25).

Wisdom in arts and science

Solomon was more than just a smart politician. He was a card-carrying member of Mensa! "Solomon's wisdom was greater than the wisdom of all the men of the East, and greater than all the wisdom of Egypt" (1 Kings 4:30). The writer singles out Solomon's accomplishments in literature (3,000 proverbs), music (1,005 songs), botany (all plants from the great cedar of Lebanon to the common hyssop), and zoology (animals, birds, reptiles, and fish). Solomon observed life at all levels, and his keen powers of observation and analysis helped him synthesize that knowledge.

Wisdom to keep peace

King David had many enemies during his lifetime, but he had also made some powerful allies. One of these was King Hiram of Tyre. Solomon sent Hiram a letter reaffirming his friendship and proposing a business deal. If Hiram would supply cedar wood for the temple, Solomon would pay Hiram and the laborers for the work. Solomon was quick to compliment Hiram on his skilled workers. "You know that we have no one so skilled in felling timber as the Sidonians" (1 Kings 5:6). Hiram agreed, and their relationship prospered. Such cooperation was no accident. "The Lord gave Solomon wisdom, just as he had promised him. There were peaceful relations between Hiram and Solomon, and the two of them made a treaty" (1 Kings 5:12).

Wisdom to exalt God

Throughout these early years Solomon never forgot the source of his wisdom and great ability. His father had wanted to build a temple for God in Jerusalem, but God had not permitted David to do so. Now, however, he dedicated himself to that task. For seven years Solomon devoted his energy, insight, and accumulated wealth to the building of a house for God. But Solomon did not let his religious devotion crowd out God. "The heavens, even the highest heaven, cannot contain you. How much less this temple I have built!" (1 Kings 8:27). Later in life he encapsulated the essence of wisdom and knowledge . . . and said it began with a proper relationship to God. "The fear of the Lord is the beginning of knowledge, but fools despise wisdom and discipline" (Proverbs 1:7).

Our first snapshot of Solomon is impressive. We see a man with a proper understanding of his limited abilities and God's abounding grace. In seeking God's wisdom, Solomon found the key that unlocked his full potential as a leader. And that wisdom helped him in all areas of life . . . from affairs of state, to observations on life, to worship.

SNAPSHOT #2:
WAYWARD SOLOMON PURSUING WIVES

The original snapshot, perhaps slightly dog-eared, is now just a memory in Solomon's photo album of life. Solomon had gazed at the picture frequently during his early days as king, but new interests entered his life to crowd out old commitments. Somewhere in the busyness of life Solomon made a wrong turn. The wisest of men was undone by a foolish mistake—one so subtle as to elude even the champion of observation.

A new snapshot shows him entering a period that pundits today could describe as his midlife crisis. At first glance the photo looks like it was taken at a large family reunion or gathering. Individual faces are hard to recognize because the photographer had to stand at a distance to get everyone in the picture. A thousand women, countless children, and one distracted man pause in their pursuit of pleasure to have their activities immortalized in this verbal snapshot of life in the royal court. What went wrong?

A careful look at this second snapshot reveals three reasons why the wisest of men made so many foolish mistakes. Solomon allowed three tiny cracks to appear in the foundation of his life, and those cracks widened to bring him crashing down. Study the snapshot carefully . . . and learn from Solomon's mistakes.

Solomon pursued forbidden pleasure

Power and prestige attract individuals who hope to profit from such connections. No doubt merchants and businessmen crowded into Solomon's palace every day seeking to secure the king's blessing—and some of his financial backing—for building projects, trading partnerships, and other ventures. The court had a cosmopolitan flair as dignitaries and envoys from countless nations around Israel sought an audience with the king to cement trade agreements and treaties.

One way to ratify a treaty between two nations was through marriage. A king would give his daughter (or another young woman from the royal family) in marriage to the king of another nation. Many of Solomon's marriages were the result of such arrangements. Evidently his Achilles' heel was his love of pleasure—especially the pleasure of beautiful women. It did not take long for these envoys to realize that one way to seal an agreement with Solomon was to give him a lovely young woman in marriage as part of the bargain.

The Bible doesn't mince words about Solomon's weakness. "King Solomon, however, loved many foreign women . . . He had seven hundred wives of royal birth and three hundred concubines, and his wives led him astray" (1 Kings 11:1, 3). Solomon lived life full throttle, and he had the resources to support his craving for good things. In the book of Ecclesiastes Solomon confesses, "I denied myself nothing my eyes desired; I refused my heart no pleasure" (Ecclesiastes 2:10).

Pleasure itself is not wrong, but it can turn one's eyes away from the Lord. Solomon became more intent on gratifying himself than on pleasing God. A tiny crack appeared in the foundation of Solomon's life, and it grew in proportion to the size of his harem.

Solomon ignored God's Word

Pleasure by itself is not wrong. Joy in life is a gift from God, who didn't intend for us to live our lives in misery! But in pursuing pleasure one must remain within the bounds of God's Word. On two key points Solomon chose to ignore specific prohibitions found in God's Word—and his disobedience in these two areas produced the second crack in his foundation.

In 1 Kings 11 the author sadly records Solomon's marriages to women from those nations around Israel. "They were from nations about which the Lord had told the Israelites, 'You must not intermarry with them, because they will surely turn your hearts after their gods.' Nevertheless, Solomon held fast to them in love" (1 Kings 11:2).

Perhaps Solomon struggled when the first of these foreign women arrived with the envoy from a neighboring state.

At the time Solomon was still living in the palace built by his father, David, perched on the northern edge of the still-small city of Jerusalem. Perhaps the walls of his new palace—and God's temple—were rising on the hill just to his north, the limestone glowing a golden white in the setting sun. The camels belched out protests as they were forced to kneel so their riders could dismount. The colorful robes of the messenger contrasted with the more utilitarian dress of the armed escort. And following behind was a young woman—the daughter of a neighboring king—dressed in the finest linen. As the envoy fawned over Solomon and described the mutual benefits of the proposed treaty, Solomon barely listened. Instead, his eyes kept moving back to take in the form and beauty of this remarkable woman who stood in his royal court. Surely God wasn't referring to *this* woman when He made such a prohibition against having foreign wives, or else why would God have made her so beautiful?

No doubt Solomon used his great intellect to construct several rationalizations for why God would consider this marriage to be an exception. But in the end he deliberately decided to disobey God's Word and follow the lust of his heart.

Somewhat later in life Solomon came to a sad realization. "All man's efforts are for his mouth, yet his appetite is never satisfied" (Ecclesiastes 6:7). And Solomon had an appetite for beautiful women. In Deuteronomy 17:17 God commanded Israel's future kings to guard their hearts. "He must not take many wives, or his heart will be led astray." Solomon must have known this command, but as each new woman arrived in his royal court, he rationalized that "just one more wife" wouldn't make a great difference. (After all, God had not set a specific number, had He?) I wonder how long Solomon lived before he woke up one day and realized he had accumulated a thousand wives and concubines.

Solomon allowed his love for God to grow cold

Solomon's pursuit of pleasure and his "benign neglect" of God's Word caused a subtle transformation in his own life. This crack in his moral foundation was the most insidious because it happened so slowly he never saw the change until it was too late. But over time his love for God grew cold, and his heart grew callous. "As Solomon grew old, his wives turned his heart after other gods, and his heart was not fully devoted to the Lord his God, as the heart of David his father had been" (1 Kings 11:4).

Solomon began his reign by following the Lord, but his heart had become dulled by success. He started well, but he finished poorly. Part of living wisely is realizing that temptations can take different forms as we grow older. The crucible of conflict that brings us closer to God in our youth often grows cold later in life. Our wealth multiplies, our reputation becomes established, our circle of friends increases . . . and the temptation to rely on ourselves instead of God grows. *Recognizing* the pleasures that allure us, *remaining* obedient to God's Word, and *maintaining* a warm relationship with the Lord are three wise actions that will help keep us faithful to God as we grow older. Solomon neglected all three . . . and he awoke one day to find that the wise young king had become a foolish old man.

SNAPSHOT #3:
OLD SOLOMON EXPLAINING THE WORLD

Shoulders stooped, bony fingers trembling slightly, Solomon waved his arm in a way that signaled for us to follow as he shuffled into the next room. There, taking a seat in front of a fire to ward off the numbing chill of Jerusalem's winter, Israel's aging monarch showed once again that though his body had grown old, his mind was still nimble. Staring out a window at nothing in particular, he carefully opened the photo album of his mind and mentally flipped through the pages of his life.

Solomon's photo album of life was nearly full. Some of the early images were faded and worn—the subject of the photos barely recognizable. The more recent pages contained dark, shadowy images that lacked the brightness so evident in the earlier ones. How could a life that started with so much promise end in such despair? This was the mystery of life we wanted Solomon to explain.

His opening words rattled us. "Meaningless! Meaningless! . . . Utterly meaningless! Everything is meaningless!" (Ecclesiastes 1:2). The man of unparalleled intellect had set out to understand the meaning of life as we know it—and his conclusion was that life by itself is empty and hollow. Like a soap bubble that glistens in the sun, life appears to have substance and meaning until you try to grasp it. The second you get your hand around it, it disappears and leaves you empty.

Was this the cynical whining of a "bitter old man"? Or were Solomon's observations profound words of wisdom that can help us live wisely today? Many have assumed the former is true, but Solomon argues for the latter. The book of Ecclesiastes is Solomon's final photograph in his album of life, and it's a photographic masterpiece that captures the essence of life itself.

Solomon has no need to gloss over his failures in life. His self-portrait in Ecclesiastes shows every wart and wrinkle. His original God-given wisdom combines with the insight he gained from life's "school of hard knocks." The result is a photograph of life as it really is, not a touched-up version.

Solomon began his portrait by recounting everything he had done to find meaning in life as it's lived here on earth. The list is impressive.

Get a good education!

Solomon began his reign as a mental "Superman" . . . with powers far beyond those of most mortals. It was just natural that the first item on his "to do" list was to figure out (using his fantastic powers of wisdom and observation) how life worked. "I devoted myself to study and to explore by wisdom all that is done under heaven" (Ecclesiastes 1:13). Bad mistake! The more he learned, the more he realized the futility of his ultimate goal. It was, he concluded, "a chasing after the wind."

In the thousands of years since Solomon, millions of individuals have devoted their lives to advancing knowledge. The more we know, the more we realize no one person can possibly understand how all life works. Scientists push the outer limits of knowledge by concentrating on ever-narrower fields of specialization. This is the only way they can possibly learn all the knowledge available that is relevant to their research. As someone wryly observed, "We know more and more about less and less, until eventually we will know everything about nothing." Only God can know everything about everything. Though education is helpful, no one person will ever gain enough knowledge to understand all of life. To think we can is futility.

MODERN SOCIETY PERPETUATES THE MYTH THAT THE ESSENCE OF LIFE IS FOUND IN THE PURSUIT OF PLEASURE.

Pursue pleasure!

Solomon didn't take long to switch his focus. If education can't supply the meaning of life, perhaps he could discover life's true meaning in the pursuit of pleasure. "You only go around once in life, and you've got to grab for all the gusto you can get!" may have become Solomon's motto at this point.

His experiments ran the gamut: pleasure and laughter (Ecclesiastes 2:1–2); mood-altering drugs (2:3), material possessions (2:4–7), wealth (2:8a), sex (2:8b), and personal influence (2:9). Then he stopped to evaluate everything he had tried. His conclusion: "Everything was meaningless, a chasing after the wind; nothing was gained under the sun" (2:11).

Modern society perpetuates the myth that the essence of life is found in the pursuit of pleasure. Solomon reached the point where he "had it all" only to discover that it wasn't enough to bring meaning and purpose to life. Most today are not wise enough to know they are running down a dead-end street.

Work hard!

Solomon's third attempt to find meaning in life took a more biblical approach. One purpose God assigned humanity was to exercise dominion over creation, and this included physical activity. God put Adam and Eve "in the Garden of Eden to work it and take care of it" (Genesis 2:15). Perhaps the real meaning to life, Solomon reasoned, came through "good old-fashioned hard work." Like many today, he looked for life's meaning in his work.

But Solomon's wisdom brought two troubling observations. First, "the work that is done under the sun was grievous to me. All of it is meaningless, a chasing after the wind" (Ecclesiastes 2:17). Sometimes work is monotonous. Sometimes life rewards diligence and hard work with failure. Sometimes work is a constant battle with unappreciative bosses, jealous coworkers, and petty bureaucrats. Work brings as much grief as it does joy.

Second, the one doing the work doesn't always enjoy the benefits. "I hated all the things I had toiled for under the sun, because I must leave them to the one who comes after me. And who knows whether he will be a wise man or a fool? Yet he will have control over all the work into which I have poured my effort and skill under the sun" (Ecclesiastes 2:18–19). Perhaps Solomon had his own son Rehoboam in mind. This foolish son soon split apart the kingdom his father had worked so hard to build. No doubt Solomon had seen the seeds of irresponsibility growing in his son and could anticipate the unpleasant results.

Some individuals work hard throughout life, putting up with grief, misery, and other frustrations to gain the material benefits hard work can bring. But they wake up one day to realize their spouses and children are strangers. They have gained material possessions but forfeited the relationships that really mattered. Others work hard to provide for themselves and their children and work themselves into an early grave. Rather than being a means to an end, work becomes an end in itself and exacts a harsh toll from those who have allowed it to enslave them. Bottom line: work did not bring the satisfaction and meaning Solomon had hoped.

SO WHAT BRINGS MEANING TO LIFE?

Does the book of Ecclesiastes contain nothing more than the angry words of a bitter man who realized too late he had squandered his life? The answer is a resounding No! The portrait is not flattering, but Solomon must be brutally honest or the alluring glitz and glitter of life itself will crowd out the truth of his words. As hard as they are to hear, Solomon's observations on life have the ring of reality. They are words of wisdom from a man who can speak from experience.

Solomon summarizes his wisdom for life in two basic statements. Instead of trying to "unscrew the inscrutable," (a) enjoy the life God has given you and (b) trust and obey the God who does understand the meaning of life.

Enjoy life

One key to living wisely in an uncertain world is to learn how to be satisfied with what God does supply. As a wise instructor, Solomon reemphasizes this theme throughout his book.

"A man can do nothing better than to eat and drink and find satisfaction in his work. This too, I see, is from the hand of God, for without him, who can eat or find enjoyment?" (Ecclesiastes 2:24–25)

"I know that there is nothing better for men than to be happy and do good while they live. That everyone may eat and drink, and find satisfaction in all his toil—this is the gift of God." (Ecclesiastes 3:12–13)

"So I saw that there is nothing better for a man than to enjoy his work, because that is his lot. For who can bring him to see what will happen after him?" (Ecclesiastes 3:22)

"Then I realized that it is good and proper for a man to eat and drink, and to find satisfaction in his toilsome labor under the sun during the few days of life God has given him—for this is his lot. Moreover, when God gives any man wealth and possessions, and enables him to enjoy them, to accept his lot and be happy in his work— this is a gift of God." (Ecclesiastes 5:18–19)

"So I commend the enjoyment of life, because nothing is better for a man under the sun than to eat and drink and be glad. Then joy will accompany him in his work all the days of the life God has given him under the sun." (Ecclesiastes 8:15)

"Go, eat your food with gladness, and drink your wine with a joyful heart, for it is now that God favors what you do. Always be clothed in white, and always anoint your head with oil. Enjoy life with your wife, whom you love, all the days of this meaningless life that God has given you under the sun—all your meaningless days. For this is your lot in life and in your toilsome labor under the sun."
(Ecclesiastes 9:7–9)

Observe closely Solomon's advice. Life from a human perspective is uncertain. You don't know how long you will live. You don't know if your hard work will bring material success. God does have a plan for your life, but He doesn't reveal the details to you. So how does one live wisely in the midst of life's uncertainties? Solomon says one secret to a wise life is to realize these uncertainties and then to enjoy the blessings God does bestow rather than becoming angry or fearful of those things over which we have no control.

Trust and Obey God

Some have described Solomon's first piece of advice as materialistic hedonism. "Eat, drink, and be merry for tomorrow we may die!" His words could be taken that way . . . were it not for the other piece of advice Solomon adds at the very end of his journal. We must understand his advice to enjoy life in the complete context of the book. First, he has already shown that a life dedicated only to the pursuit of pleasure will result in emptiness (Ecclesiastes 2). Second, he ends the book by pointing his readers beyond the materialism of this life to the reality of God and the life to come. These two restrictions form a set of mental "bookends" that limit the meaning one can give to his other words of advice.

Solomon reached the conclusion of his book by pointing

his audience to the ultimate Source of the wisdom found within its pages. "The words of the wise are like goads, their collected sayings like firmly embedded nails—given by one Shepherd" (Ecclesiastes 12:11). What is God's final word on how to live wisely in uncertain times? "Now all has been heard; here is the conclusion of the matter: Fear God and keep his commandments, for this is the whole duty of man. For God will bring every deed into judgment, including every hidden thing, whether it is good or evil" (Ecclesiastes 12:13–14). Wisdom is remembering that God is in charge and that He will work everything out in His own way. We are not responsible to understand why everything in life happens as it does. But we are responsible to trust Him in spite of life's circumstances.

Solomon's secret to wisdom? Wisdom begins when we develop a proper relationship to God . . . recognizing our limitations and humbly following His divine directives. "The fear of the Lord is the beginning of knowledge, but fools despise wisdom and discipline" (Proverbs 1:7).

Reflect and Respond

We tend to associate wisdom with knowledge. But a wise individual is one who understands, from God's perspective, how life works. Take some time to focus on several pointed questions related to practical wisdom.

1. Are you a "workaholic"? Does work take priority over your family or your time with the Lord? If so, what can you do this week to put God and family first?
2. Memorize Proverbs 1:7 and ask God to develop His wisdom in your life as you seek to trust and obey Him.
3. If you divided your life into self-portraits (as we did with Solomon's), what would the snapshots look like up to this point?
4. Is there an area in which you're knowledgeable? How can wisdom be applied to this knowledge? What can happen when wisdom is not added to knowledge?
5. Are you enjoying the life God gave you? How is enjoyment of life connected with wisdom?

"For the foolishness of God is wiser than man's wisdom, and the weakness of God is stronger than man's strength."
(1 Corinthians 1:25)

HE WHO REIGNS WITHIN HIMSELF, AND
RULES PASSIONS, DESIRES, AND FEARS,
IS MORE THAN A KING.

—*John Milton*

A LITTLE KINGDOM I POSSESS, WHERE
THOUGHTS AND FEELINGS DWELL; AND
VERY HARD THE TASK I FIND OF
GOVERNING IT WELL.

—*Louisa May Alcott*

4

BY-LAWS OR
BYE, LAWS?:
Self-Control

Discipline is an unpopular word! At least that's the impression we give by our inability to exercise self-control. The national debate over health care stirred up strong passions on all sides, and many found it difficult to control their emotions. During President Obama's speech to Congress on health care, one congressman shouted out, "You lie!" He later apologized for his regrettable lack of self-control, but his remark illustrates the struggle we all face exercising self-control. A lack of self-discipline isn't admirable and can be embarrassing!

Parents who desire to fashion their children into responsible adults are painfully aware of the struggle over self-control. Parenting is the process of moving children from external discipline to internal self-control . . . and at times the process seems to move at a snail's pace.

But why worry about self-control? Our society champions an individual's right to freedom and self-expression. "If it feels good, do it!" "Have it your way!" "Just do it!" Doesn't too much emphasis on self-control stifle creativity, inhibit freedom, and squeeze the fun out of life? Not necessarily.

True self-control doesn't hinder freedom—it promotes it. Alcoholics have no self-control in their consumption of alcohol—and it enslaves them. Compulsive gamblers have no control over their impulse to gamble—and it destroys their financial security. Those addicted to pornography have no control over their sexual addiction—and it destroys their ability to maintain healthy relationships with those of the opposite sex.

Absolute freedom without any self-control, will *always* produce chaos. Self-control provides the boundaries inside which true freedom and creativity can flourish. It brings a maturity that allows an individual to say no to some things so he or she can say yes to those things that are more significant, helpful, or necessary.

In his runaway bestseller *The 7 Habits of Highly Effective People*, Stephen Covey stressed the importance of commitment and self-control. He explained that as we make and keep commitments—even minor ones—we begin to establish an inner integrity that gives us the awareness of self-control and the courage and strength to accept more of the responsibility for our own lives. By making and keeping promises to ourselves and others, our honor becomes greater than our moods.[12]

EAT YOUR VEGETABLES!

All parents learn the "airplane method" of feeding little children. The child, like a condemned prisoner, is strapped into the chair. On the table, just out of reach, are the jars of strained, pureed—and otherwise mutilated—vegetables that no self-respecting adult would ever eat. Then we try to trick our children into eating the necessary amount of pureed spinach and squash by saying as excitedly as possible, "Here comes the plane into the hangar! Open wide!"

The child grows, the style of chair changes, and the plate and utensils become more "adult" in appearance. But the hassle over vegetables continues. "No dessert until you eat those peas and carrots!" The struggle still remains to get children to do what they *need* to do rather than what they *want* to do. Given a reasonable choice, few children would ever choose peas and carrots over cookies and ice cream without some form of "encouragement." The war to establish self-discipline is a series of such battles.

EXTERNAL CONTROLS

Self-discipline sounds great in theory, but try putting it into practice! Try telling a hormone-driven eighteen-year-old boy to control his thought life. Or try telling the frazzled mother of an energetic two-year-old to control her frustration. Life's pressures and difficulties sometimes catch us in their vise-like grip and squeeze until we feel as though we will explode. Every nerve ending seems rubbed raw, every ounce of strength sapped by these problems that hang on us like weights and suck out our strength like leeches. How can we develop self-control in a world that seems to do everything possible to titillate, tempt, test, and try our patience at every turn?

One wrong response to the struggle over self-control is to set up legalistic barriers—using external controls to regulate an internal problem. After Ayatollah Khomeini and his Islamic fundamentalist allies took control in Iran, they imposed strict Muslim law and external controls over behavior. Women were no longer allowed to dress in "provocative" Western styles. Instead, the authorities required them to wear the *chador*, a dark robe that covered the entire body. Possession of pornography became a crime punishable by death.

Did such draconian measures solve the problem of sexual self-control? No! The regime still struggles vainly to plug the many loopholes in the law and impose their external moral standards. They even banned satellite dishes because thousands of homes were receiving X-rated movies and other sexually explicit programs through these dishes.

External controls do not provide a long-term change in behavior.

UNDER PAUL'S WING

The essential struggles we face have not changed through the years because human nature has not changed. Two millennia ago the apostle Paul wrote to a young man in western Turkey struggling with some of the same problems facing us today. Timothy served as Paul's young protégé. He traveled with Paul on his journeys and learned much from this great apostle.

Life with Paul must have been both exciting and stressful. Paul's own description of his ministry leaves no doubt it was not for the faint of heart:

> "I have worked much harder, been in prison more frequently, been flogged more severely, and been exposed to death again and again. Five times I received from the Jews the forty lashes minus one. Three times I was beaten with rods, once I was stoned, three times I was shipwrecked, I spent a night and a day in the open sea, I have been constantly on the move. I have been in danger from rivers, in danger from bandits, in danger from my own countrymen, in danger from Gentiles; in danger in the city, in danger in the country, in danger at sea; and in danger from false brothers." (2 Corinthians 11:23–26)

Traveling with Paul was like serving on the front lines in a war. Always on the go. Always in harm's way. One hair-raising adventure after another. Paul had a mission from God, and Timothy did his best to keep up with his dynamic mentor. But being around Paul was intimidating. And Timothy was painfully aware of each of his perceived shortcomings.

THE NUMBER OF BELIEVERS IN JESUS CHRIST HAD GROWN TO THE POINT WHERE THE AUTHORITIES IN ROME WERE NOW TAKING NOTICE.

Timothy must have felt like the odd-man-out of church leadership. In a society that valued age, associating it with wisdom, Timothy was a mere lad (1 Timothy 4:12). In a culturally segregated society, Timothy was the product of a religiously and racially mixed marriage—a believing Jewish mother and a pagan Gentile father (Acts 16:1). In a church that needed vigorous, powerful leaders, Timothy was timid and subject to frequent illness (1 Timothy 5:23; 2 Timothy 1:6–8).

Imagine Timothy's concern when the apostle Paul left him alone in Ephesus as Paul's official representative. Paul expected Timothy to handle some serious problems that threatened to fragment this strategic church. To add additional stress, times were tough for all churches in the Roman Empire. The number of believers in Jesus Christ had grown to the point where the authorities in Rome were now taking notice. Sometime after leaving Timothy in Ephesus the apostle Paul was arrested, taken to Rome, and imprisoned by the Roman government for a second time. This imprisonment ended with his execution.

Timothy inherited a church that was floundering because of false teaching and defections from the faith. Some advocated rigid, external obedience to restrictive laws as the way to achieve self-control and acceptance with God. "They forbid people to marry and order them to abstain from certain foods" (1 Timothy 4:3). Others promoted self-centered philosophies based on vain speculation. Paul expected young, struggling Timothy to model the message of biblical self-control to these people. To do so, Paul shared three specific pointers with Timothy for developing this character trait in himself and others.

POINTER #1:
FALL IN LOVE WITH JESUS CHRIST

A magical transformation takes place in a young man's life sometime during his teenage years. Those "yucky girls" he had once tried to avoid suddenly become interesting, exciting . . . desirable! It's as if the poles of a magnet suddenly reversed. The shapely cootie-carriers that used to repel now seem irresistibly attractive. That's amoré!

Love also causes changes in actions and attitudes. A young man in love starts caring about his overall appearance—his clothing, his hair, his complexion. Moms stand in awe, mouths hanging open, as their sons *willingly* assume responsibility for their personal appearance.

The desire to please someone we love is a powerful motivational force. The patriarch Jacob worked for seven long years to gain permission to marry Rachel, "but they seemed like only a few days to him because of his love for her" (Genesis 29:20). If you love someone deeply, you willingly limit your freedom because your greater desire is to please them. Self-control flows easily from a heart of love.

The apostle Paul understood this pointer for developing self-control. Leaving Timothy in Ephesus, Paul urged him to stop the spread of false teaching. Timothy was to promote God's true message in the church. "The goal of this command is love, which comes from a pure heart and a good conscience and a sincere faith" (1 Timothy 1:5).

Paul knew firsthand the power of love. As a zealous Pharisee on the road to Damascus he experienced God's love . . . and it changed his life. Paul unflinchingly described himself before he knew Jesus Christ as "a blasphemer and a persecutor and a violent man" (1 Timothy 1:13). God extended His grace to someone deserving only of judgment, and Paul's debt of love motivated him to serve his Lord.

How much do you love the Lord? Another apostle, John, reminded his readers of the order in which love develops. "We love because he [God] first loved us" (1 John 4:19). The more you realize the depth of God's love for you . . . a love so deep He willingly sent His Son to die for your sins . . . the more you will grow in your love for Him. And the more you love Him, the more willing you will be to make those changes in your life that will please Him.

POINTER #2:
LEARN AND LIVE OUT THE WORD OF GOD

Racquetball is a fast-paced sport that could be described as kamikaze tennis! Up to four people stand in a small room swinging short racquets at a hollow rubber ball. The ball bounces wildly off the floor, ceiling, and four walls. Each player tries to hit the ball off the front wall in a way that denies the other player(s) an opportunity to make a return shot.

The secret in racquetball is knowing where the ball will bounce after hitting the front wall . . . and anticipating your opponent's next shot. A strong, quick, but inexperienced racquetball player will usually lose to a more knowledgeable opponent, even if that opponent is older, slower, and weaker. Knowledge and skill are more important than strength and speed. Mastering the disciplines of the game gives a player an edge.

Paul wrote to Timothy to give him the knowledge and skill he needed to direct the church at Ephesus. Timothy needed to master the skills essential for becoming an effective leader. In 1 Timothy 4 Paul shared with Timothy the vital link between self-discipline and the Word of God.

He began by reminding Timothy he had been "brought up in the truths of the faith and of the good teaching that you have followed" (1 Timothy 4:6). Before Timothy could serve as a "good minister of Christ Jesus" (4:6), he had to know the truth of God's Word. Mastering the fundamentals is essential for developing self-discipline.

But knowing and teaching the truth of God's Word is not

enough. The truth must move from our head . . . to our heart . . . to our hands. Timothy was not only to "command and teach" God's truth, Paul also expected him to "set an example for the believers" (1 Timothy 4:11–12).

Paul listed five specific areas in which Timothy needed to develop self-discipline. Each is important.

- **Speech** Be an example in what you say
- **Life** Be an example in what you do
- **Love** Be an example in how you help others
- **Faith** Be an example in how you trust God
- **Purity** Be an example in how you relate to the opposite sex

I suspect young Timothy's throat tightened and his heart started racing in his chest as he read through the list. Paul wanted self-discipline in *every* area of life, and Timothy was keenly aware of his own struggles and limitations. How could he possibly live up to all these requirements?

Paul's answer follows. "Until I come, devote yourself to the public reading of Scripture, to preaching and to teaching" (1 Timothy 4:13). As Timothy immersed himself in God's Word, he would find the answers he needed to develop self-discipline—in himself, and in the lives of God's people in Ephesus.

God's Word provides the knowledge we need to live in a way that pleases God. The more we study God's Word and make it part of our thought process, the more we will be able to live lives characterized by self-discipline.

WE NEED A KNOWL-EDGE OF GOD'S WORD IF WE HOPE TO LIVE SUCCESSFULLY.

When my two children were much younger, I once took them to "play" racquetball. They swung wildly at the ball and ran to the right as the ball bounced off the wall toward the left. They had fun . . . but they didn't play racquetball! They lacked the basic knowledge of how to play the game. And without that knowledge they could not be successful.

Our Christian lives are the same. We need a knowledge of God's Word if we hope to live successfully. It's hard to exercise self-discipline if we don't know which areas of our life we need to develop. Only God's Word gives us that truth.

POINTER #3:
DON'T FALL INTO LEGALISM

Our "hurry-up" society has mastered the thirty-second sound bite. As life becomes more hectic we search for easy answers. Many citizens choose their elected leaders based on television, radio, and Internet ads that are long on style . . . and short on substance.

We expect reporters to summarize national and international news to the point where we can learn what's happening in the world almost in real time, especially with breaking news online coming to our computers and cell phones.

We take a similar approach to biblical self-discipline. Self-control takes so long to develop the old-fashioned way. Can't we reduce God's expectations for our lives to the "top ten" or "big five" commands He wants us to follow? It would be so much easier to live a life of self-discipline if all we had to remember was "Don't drink, smoke, or chew . . . or go with girls who do!"

A ready-made list of dos and don'ts for living the Christian life sounds inviting, but the results are devastating. Eventually the list becomes more important than God's Word.

The Pharisees started out with a noble desire. They wanted to build a hedge around God's Word lest they accidentally violate a command and sin against God. Their specific lists of dos and don'ts were fences designed to help them and their followers stay inside God's Law.

Unfortunately, by the time of Jesus their list of dos and don'ts had grown to the point where they harmed those who tried to keep them. Jesus reserved some of His harshest condemnations for those who preached such legalism. "They tie up heavy loads and put them on men's shoulders, but they themselves are not willing to lift a finger to move them" (Matthew 23:4). In the same passage Jesus called the Pharisees "hypocrites," "blind guides," "blind fools," "whitewashed tombs," "snakes," and a "brood of vipers"! As He spoke these words Jesus' followers could look from Jerusalem toward the Mount of Olives and see ornate mausoleums—intricately carved and painted white, but filled with decaying bodies. And just beyond was the Judean Wilderness with its deadly snakes and scorpions.

Why such harsh words? Jesus condemned those who promote legalism because legalism inevitably does just the opposite of what it sets out to do. Instead of helping define the Word of God, it replaces the Word of God with human rules. Instead of providing freedom to do what is right, it enslaves in a system too burdensome to bear. Instead of promoting righteousness, it fosters hypocritical pride. Instead of leading to life, it ultimately results in death.

Don't get me wrong. The opposite of legalism is *not* lawlessness . . . it's the standards of righteousness found in God's Word. Legalism takes the Word of God and adds to it. It substitutes specific human rules for those ordained by God.

I see two very specific differences between legalism and the standards set by God. First, legalism tries to set tighter boundaries than God imposes in His Word. God's Word told Israel to "remember the Sabbath day by keeping it holy" (Exodus 20:8). The legalism of the Pharisees told Israel how they could eat on the Sabbath (Matthew 12:1–2), what they could—and could not—carry on the Sabbath (John 5:10), and how far they could walk on the Sabbath (Acts 1:12). They added shackles to the Law of God.

Second, legalism leads to the belief that keeping a specific list of laws will make a person righteous. But God's Word says a person should try to live a righteous life because God has *already* made him or her righteous. Legalism holds out the promise of earning favor with God by following a set of rules. Biblical self-discipline encourages individuals to obey God's Word so their lives can match their settled position as God's children.

Legalism is not something new. The Pharisees practiced it in Christ's day, and some individuals tried to impose it on the church in Ephesus. Paul warned Timothy of the danger of substituting legalism for self-discipline. The false teachers in Ephesus stressed obedience to the law (1 Timothy 1:7–10). Paul reminded Timothy that "law is made not for the righteous but for lawbreakers and rebels, the ungodly and sinful, the unholy and irreligious" (1:9).

Law can help hold evil in check, but it can't produce righteousness. Law puts criminals in prison . . . but it doesn't make those who are already righteous more godly.

Paul reminded Timothy of the motives behind many individuals who promote legalism. "Such teachings come through hypocritical liars, whose consciences have been seared as with a hot iron" (1 Timothy 4:2). Harsh words, but true. People who add their standards of right and wrong to the Word of God are usurping the place of God.

Paul gave two specific examples of the legalism creeping

into the church at Ephesus. "They forbid people to marry and order them to abstain from certain foods" (1 Timothy 4:3). Perhaps these teachers thought that forbidding all marriage would solve the problem of sexual immorality. It didn't! Perhaps they thought a list of "forbidden foods" would keep them from offending others. It wouldn't! What these additional lists of rules accomplished was to take the very things God created as good and call them evil. Legalism was *not* the route Timothy needed to take to develop self-discipline.

Get on God's Exercise Program

Though Timothy had faithfully served with Paul for nearly a decade, he still needed to continue developing self-control in his life. Paul challenged him to "train yourself to be godly" (1 Timothy 4:7). The process takes time . . . and effort.

Life is a marathon not a sprint, and it requires discipline and endurance. The author of Hebrews reminds us of this important principle, and his words of challenge and encouragement are a good way to end our focus on self-control. "Therefore, since we are surrounded by such a great cloud of witnesses, let us throw off everything that hinders and the sin that so easily entangles, and let us run with perseverance the race marked out for us. Let us fix our eyes on Jesus, the author and perfecter of our faith" (Hebrews 12:1–2a).

Reflect and Respond

Self-control is a by-product of God's ministry in our lives. "But the fruit of the Spirit is . . . self-control" (Galatians 5:22–23). We can aid in the process as we come to know and love God and His Word.

1. How much do you love the Lord? Read Philippians 2 and pause to think about all Jesus did for you. Then stop to thank the Lord and express your love to God.
2. Are you spending time in God's Word? If not, consider committing to reading at least one chapter in the Bible every day. You could start with Paul's letters to Timothy.
3. Are you relying on following rules instead of pursuing Christ? How can you grow closer to Him?
4. Are there areas in which you need to practice self-discipline? What is one step can you take today?
5. Memorize Galatians 5:22–23 and compare your life to the "fruit of the Spirit."

"Train yourself to be godly. For physical training is of some value, but godliness has value for all things, holding promise for both the present life and the life to come." (1 Timothy 4:7–8)

GOD HAS WISELY KEPT US IN THE DARK
CONCERNING FUTURE EVENTS AND
RESERVED FOR HIMSELF THE
KNOWLEDGE OF THEM, THAT HE MAY
TRAIN US UP IN A DEPENDENCE UPON
HIMSELF AND A CONTINUED READINESS
FOR EVERY EVENT.

—*Matthew Henry*

5

CAN I DEPEND ON GOD?:
Trust

FROM BEAVER CLEAVER TO BART SIMPSON

Western society has been rocked by a profound spiritual, social, and moral shift that began in the 1950s. Much of the shift in the United States can be attributed to the post-World War II "baby boom" generation. In contrast to their parents, baby boomers—and those who have followed them—came to adulthood:

- fearing nuclear annihilation and global warming rather than the Great Depression or fascism
- opposing war (in Vietnam, Iraq, and Afghanistan) rather than supporting World War II
- Gaining information visually (through television and the Internet) rather than through listening to the radio or reading a newspaper
- distrusting, rather than respecting, those in authority.

The Beaver Cleavers of years gone by have become today's Bart Simpsons. And along the way we lost our ability to trust.

WHOM CAN YOU TRUST?

During the Great Depression President Franklin Roosevelt's "fireside chats" offered comfort and assurance to Americans awash in a sea of uncertainty. The president cared. The president was doing something. The president would eventually take care of our problems.

The scandal we came to call Watergate shattered that sense of trust for those who remember living through it. In subsequent years a string of allegations and exposés have further eroded citizens' trust in those who govern the nation. Trust a politician? You've got to be kidding!

If we can't trust politicians, whom can we trust? How about the police, our appointed guardians of law and order? Nearly every week brings another story about an alleged police beating of a suspect while in custody. At one time people would believe the police officer's account over that of a suspect without question. After all it was the word of the police (whom we were taught to trust) against the word of someone who had been arrested. But then individuals with cell phones recorded some of those incidents, and we felt our trust had been violated. Trust the police? Now we aren't so sure.

In our desperate search for trust we turn to the church. God's servants ought to be the most trustworthy individuals around, because they represent the One who "is called Faithful and True" (Revelation 19:11). And those who claim to know and speak for God anger us most when we read new allegations of sexual impropriety or gross financial misconduct. Our sense of cynicism grows when someone who claims to be a "man of God" violates our trust.

I recently visited a church torn apart by a minister who violated the congregation's trust. Though he had only been at the church for a few years, his charm, confidence, and persuasive speech had mesmerized most members. He skillfully led the church through a series of strategic moves that appeared to be very successful. The congregation was growing, giving was increasing, and the pastor's reputation was spreading. This was "the" church for the community.

Then someone just happened to show up at the pastor's study unannounced, uninvited, and unanticipated . . . and caught the pastor in the arms of a woman who was not his wife. The congregation was shocked, devastated, and angry. They felt humiliated as word of the pastor's sordid affair spread through the community.

Now the pastor is gone, his family is shattered. The

church's reputation in the town remains tarnished, and the congregation is only a fraction of its former size. And those who chose to remain find it difficult to trust the new pastor.

It's tragic for a local church to go through such an experience, but when a story of someone in a prominent place of Christian leadership makes the national news, it only serves to fuel the nonbelievers' sense that religious people are not trustworthy.

Politicians. Police. Pastors. Three specific groups of individuals given authority and responsibility. Three groups whom we expected to be trustworthy . . . but who have experienced notable failures in recent years. No wonder we are so cynical and untrusting! Can we trust anyone?

In God We Trust

My struggles with trust took a dramatic turn the year I graduated from college. I was graduating in May, getting married in June, and moving to Texas in August to begin graduate studies. As spring approached I began questioning my decision to move. How did I know this was what God wanted me to do? How could I be sure God would take care of me? Was this a wise move for Kathy and me? One of my problems was that I knew *no one* in Texas.

We packed everything we owned in a 4 x 6 U-Haul—and most of that was books. As the time drew near for us to leave, we scraped together all our resources. After paying off our college debts we had just enough money to drive to Texas, rent a small apartment, buy a few weeks' worth of groceries, and pay for our first semester of seminary tuition. Hardly a nest egg!

How could we make such a move? Looking back at it today it still seems rather remarkable. And yet I remember very specifically what gave me the peace, the faith, and the trust to make such a move at that time. Earlier that spring I had started praying and asking God to be very specific in showing me what He wanted me to do. I had applied to graduate school, and I told Him that if He wanted me to go to Texas, He would need to make it very clear.

During the time I was praying I was also reading through the book of Hebrews in my time alone with God. A few weeks after I asked God for a specific sense of direction I came to Hebrews 11. One verse jumped off the page. "By faith Abraham, when called to go to a place he would later receive as his inheritance, obeyed and went, even though he did not know where he was going" (Hebrews 11:8).

God used that verse in my life to teach me the meaning of faith and trust. Abraham was a man of faith who, when God directed him to do something, obeyed even if he didn't fully understand all the details of what God was asking. He trusted God enough to know God could take care of the details. That was the lesson I had to master. Was my God big enough to take care of Kathy and me when we moved to Texas? The answer, we discovered, was a resounding Yes! God took us through that time and helped us grow very dramatically in our trust of Him.

FAITH IS THE ABILITY TO TRUST IN GOD AND HIS PROMISES BEFORE WE SEE THEM COME TO PASS.

Not that it was always easy . . . For years I saved the check register for that first year in seminary. There were times when we had less than five dollars in our checking account with more than a week left till payday. (We ate a *lot* of macaroni and cheese!) But in the midst of those difficult times God showed us repeatedly that He could—and would—meet our needs. We learned to trust, because as we stepped out in faith we found God was dependable.

By Faith Abraham . . .

Hebrews 11 is often called God's "Hall of Faith." The chapter mentions "faith" twenty-two times and illustrates it from the lives of at least sixteen specific individuals. The writer begins the chapter by defining the essence of faith. "Now faith is being sure of what we hope for and certain of what we do not see" (11:1). Faith is the ability to trust in God and His promises before we see them come to pass.

In selecting Abraham the writer chose an important example for his Jewish-Christian readers. Abraham was the physical and spiritual father of all Jews. And he lived a life characterized by faith. The author of Hebrews used Abraham to teach three specific lessons on faith.

Faith follows when God calls

Our first glimpse of Abraham gives no hint of his later greatness. Had Ur of the Chaldees had a high school, the senior class would not have nominated Abraham as "Most Likely to Succeed." Abram (Abraham's original name) was one of three sons born into a pagan family. His father "worshiped other gods" (Joshua 24:2). Ur, the city of his birth, was a center for the worship of the moon-god. Abraham's brother Haran died, and Abraham assumed responsibility for raising his surviving son. Abram married Sarai (Sarah's original name), but their inability to have children marred the marriage. Nothing in his background set Abraham apart as a remarkable man of faith.

What transformed Abraham? The Bible recorded the answer three different times.

- "The Lord had said to Abram, 'Leave your country, your people and your father's household and go to the land I will show you.' . . . So Abram left, as the Lord had told him." (Genesis 12:1, 4)

- "The God of glory appeared to our father Abraham while he was still in Mesopotamia, before he lived in Haran. 'Leave your country and your people,' God said, 'and go to the land I will show you.' So he left the land of the Chaldeans and settled in Haran. After the death of his father, God sent him to this land." (Acts 7:2–4)
- "By faith Abraham, when called to go to a place he would later receive as his inheritance, obeyed and went, even though he did not know where he was going." (Hebrews 11:8)

What set Abraham apart and made him such a remarkable example of faith? In each passage the answer is very simple: he followed when God called. No excuses. No equivocating. No hesitation. When God said to move, Abraham packed the tent! And this was no small undertaking. Abraham had servants as well as flocks and herds. They would require provisions, grazing land, water. Abraham was responsible for the welfare of hundreds (Genesis 14:14). Some would call Abraham's response a "blind leap of faith." But was it really? No, for two reasons.

First, Abraham was responding to a personal encounter with God. God first revealed Himself to Abraham, and Abraham's actions were in response to God's revelation. Every time the Bible records this event, God's summons precedes Abraham's response.

Second, though Abraham may not have known his immediate destination, he had supreme confidence in his eternal Guide. The writer of Hebrews puts Abraham's faith in perspective. Though Abraham "did not know where he was going" as he journeyed from Mesopotamia to the land of Canaan, he saw this trip as a small part of his larger journey of faith. He could live with uncertainty and impermanence in this life because "he was looking forward to the city with foundations, whose architect and builder is God" (Hebrews 11:10).

I thought about the importance of a guide as our tour bus hurtled around a sharp bend on a little-used road in Israel. I was leading twenty-five students on a study tour, but this day was unique. Normally I guide our group, but today we had a local Israeli guide. Even the bus driver had not driven the roads we were now on! In fact, some of the "roads" were nothing more than dirt tracks scraped from the rocky hillside. In the politically volatile Middle East one wrong turn could send our bus with Israeli license plates into a West Bank Arab village where we would be uninvited . . . and unwelcomed.

The bus driver was an Israeli Arab who is both a skillful driver and a personal friend. He and I exchanged glances, and I could tell he was nervous. Our lives were in the hands of a the guide, a man we just met for the first time the previous evening. We had to trust in his ability to lead us to the promised destination.

The dirt road wound its way up the side of a mountain. On top we scrambled off the bus for a spectacular view. Walking around the top of the mountain we could see the Jordan Valley where Abraham first crossed into the land of Canaan . . . the Wadi Faria he followed past Tirzah into the hill country . . . and the city of Shechem with its twin peaks of Mount Ebal and Mount Gerazim where he first settled. The guide then told us we were standing on Elon Moreh, the first location in the land where God appeared to Abraham (Genesis 12:6–7). The reddish soil and white limestone rock hinted at the richness of the land, though it was now largely covered in thorns and brush. But below, in the valley, we could see rows of fruit trees and fields of ripening wheat that showed how productive the land could be when it was properly nurtured and cultivated.

I had no idea what roads our bus was on or where they would lead. But I wasn't worried because the guide leading us had an excellent reputation . . . and he knew where he was going. In the same way Abraham started on a journey before he knew the destination. But his faith was not some blind leap in the dark because he trusted the Guide who was directing his steps.

Faith trusts when God promises

The writer of Hebrews provides a second example of Abraham's faith. God not only asked Abraham to follow Him into the unknown, He also asked him to believe the impossible. Abraham was seventy-five years old when he and Sarah began their journey to the Promised Land. At a time of life when many men are content to reminisce about the old days, Abraham pulled up stakes and headed west.

But one problem remained. God not only promised Abraham real estate, He also promised an heir. Not many seventy-five-year-old men with sixty-five-year-old wives worry about the location of the nearest elementary school when they move! Abraham must have struggled with the seeming absurdity of God's promise because he later says to God, "You have given me no children; so a servant in my household will be my heir" (Genesis 15:3). Hey, God! It's hard to see how I will become a "great nation" when I won't even have any children I can call my own.

God's answer startled Abraham. "This man [Abraham's servant] will not be your heir, but a son coming from your own body will be your heir." God then took Abraham outside for an astronomy lesson. "'Look up at the heavens and count the stars—if indeed you can count them.' Then he said to him, 'So shall your offspring be'" (Genesis 15:4–5). Stock up on Pampers, Abraham, you'll soon be changing a lot of diapers!

What do you do when God makes such an outlandish statement? If you're Abraham, you trust in the truth of the statement because it was spoken by God. "Abram believed the Lord, and he credited it to him as righteousness" (Genesis 15:6). Abraham accepted God's promise, though he struggled to understand fully how it could happen.

Ten years later Abraham still struggled. He and Sarah tried to "help God" by fathering a son using Sarah's Egyptian servant girl as a surrogate mother (Genesis 16). Major mistake! The resulting friction and family fighting shattered Abraham's household. Conflicts developed that extend down to today through the descendants of Isaac and Ishmael.

If Abraham had doubts about having children at seventy-five and tried to "help God" at eighty-six, imagine how he felt when he reached the ripe old age of ninety-nine. He and Sarah, for all practical purposes, had both passed the age when they could ever hope to have children. God chose that time to announce that a new addition would be arriving at Abraham's house in time for his one hundredth birthday. "As for Sarai your wife, you are no longer to call her Sarai; her name will be Sarah. I will bless her and will surely give you a son by her" (Genesis 17:15–16).

God's announcement stunned Abraham. "Will a son be born to a man a hundred years old? Will Sarah bear a child at the age of ninety?" (Genesis 17:17). Abraham was amazed . . . but he immediately started calling his wife "Sarah"! He also obeyed God's command to practice circumcision. "On that very day Abraham took . . . every male in his household, and circumcised them, as God told him" (Genesis 17:23). Abraham's willingness to change his wife's name to Sarah and to circumcise everyone in his household demonstrated his trusting response to God's promise.

The writer of Hebrews highlighted Abraham's trust in

God's promises . . . and emphasized the results. "By faith Abraham, even though he was past age—and Sarah herself was barren—was enabled to become a father because he considered him faithful who had made the promise. And so from this one man, and he as good as dead, came descendants as numerous as the stars in the sky and as countless as the sand on the seashore" (Hebrews 11:11–12).

Faith obeys when God commands

Faith is our ability to follow when God calls and to trust when God promises. But one essential element still might be lacking. Abraham's supreme demonstration of faith was his ability to obey when God commanded.

Abraham's life seemed to settle into a pattern of calm predictability. Isaac, his child of promise, was growing into a young man. The struggles with Ishmael were past. The conflicts with Canaan's kings had all been smoothed over. Life was good!

Then God threw Abraham a curve ball. "Take your son, your only son, Isaac, whom you love, and go to the region of Moriah. Sacrifice him there as a burnt offering on one of the mountains I will tell you about" (Genesis 22:2). What? Sacrifice my son? Do you know what you're asking? Abraham must have spent a sleepless night mulling over God's all-consuming command. God was asking him to give the supreme sacrifice: his only son, a son conceived by divine promise, a son deeply loved by his father.

But however great the personal fear, anxiety, and pain, Abraham obeyed God's command. "Early the next morning Abraham got up and saddled his donkey. He took with him two of his servants and his son Isaac" (Genesis 22:3). By dawn's early light Abraham set out for the place selected by God as the mountain of sacrifice.

How could Abraham obey God's command without hesitation? Some would say it was because he feared the anger of a vengeful God more than he feared the loss of his son. But such a view underestimates God's love and Abraham's faith. God designed His command to test the depth of Abraham's trust and obedience. Once Abraham had demonstrated his willingness to obey God, in spite of the consequences, God stopped Abraham from slaying his son. Instead, God provided a ram as a substitute. "[Abraham] went over and took the ram and sacrificed it as a burnt offering instead of his son" (Genesis 22:13). Though animal sacrifices existed from the beginning of fallen human history (Genesis 4:3–5), for the first time the Bible clearly speaks of one life being substituted for another. God provided a substitute so Abraham would not need to sacrifice his son.

> IF GOD'S COMMAND SEEMS REASONABLE, IF IT FITS OUR PLANS AND GOALS FOR LIFE, AND IF IT ULTIMATELY BENEFITS US, THEN WE ARE USUALLY WILLING TO OBEY.

The writer of Hebrews adds one additional element that helps explain Abraham's faith. "By faith Abraham, when God tested him, offered Isaac as a sacrifice. . . . Abraham reasoned that God could raise the dead, and figuratively speaking, he did receive Isaac back from death" (Hebrews 11:17, 19). What faith! Though Abraham had never seen, heard, or read of the resurrection of the dead, he reasoned that if God had predicted Isaac was the son of promise, then God would keep His word. If God was asking Abraham to sacrifice Isaac, God would need to restore Isaac's life to fulfill His earlier promises. Abraham could obey when God asked him to do the impossible because he had supreme confidence in God's willingness and ability to keep His word.

Are you willing to obey God? If God's command seems reasonable, if it fits our plans and goals for life, and if it ultimately benefits us, then we are usually willing to obey. But what if obedience to God runs counter to our plans, hopes, and aspirations? In those times we can obey only if we have supreme trust in the power and goodness of God. Abraham was a great example of faith because he could trust God in spite of circumstances . . . his eyes of faith could see beyond the circumstances.

But don't put Abraham on a pedestal! His faith, remarkable though it was, is not beyond your grasp. He still struggled, just as we do, with fears, frustrations, and failures. No sooner had he arrived in the "promised land" than he abandoned it during a time of famine (Genesis 12:10). After arriving in Egypt he lied about Sarah being his wife because he was afraid of being killed (Genesis 12:11–20). As many of us often do, Abraham actually told a half-truth to deceive. He claimed Sarah was his "sister," and in truth she was his half-sister. They were born to the same father but had different mothers (Genesis 20:12). But in stressing the biological identity as siblings—he neglected to mention that she was also his wife! Abraham tried to accomplish God's will through his own human effort—and he created a long-lasting family feud (Genesis 16:15; 21:8–21). In the midst of his family struggles he lied a second time about Sarah being his wife (Genesis 20:2–18)! Abraham struggled in his walk with God—just as you and I do.

So what set Abraham apart? Ultimately, it was his faith in God. Though he often failed, he still knew he could trust God. That sense of trust allowed Abraham to follow when God called him to a new land. It allowed Abraham to believe God's promises when they seemed so contrary to actual experience. And his faith allowed him to obey when God asked him to give up that which he held most dear.

THE FATHER'S SACRIFICE

We have many tests today that seek to quantify an individual's IQ (intelligence quotient). But have you ever taken a test to determine your FQ (faith quotient)? How much do you trust God?

The supreme test of Abraham's faith was his willingness to give up his only son. Though God's request seemed strange (and perhaps harsh), God was asking Abraham to do nothing more than God Himself had already decided to do. Before asking Abraham to part with his son, God had already decided to sacrifice His Son, Jesus Christ. "For God so loved the world that he gave his one and only Son, that whoever believes in him shall not perish but have eternal life" (John 3:16).

The first—and most important—step of faith anyone can take is to place his trust for eternal life in Jesus Christ. The Bible teaches that "all have sinned and fall short of the glory of God" (Romans 3:23). Everyone has violated God's perfect standards of righteous thought and action. The Bible also says, "The wages of sin is death" (Romans 6:23). God, in His perfect justice and holiness, must exclude from heaven all who fall short of His absolute standards of perfection. Anyone not perfectly free of sin receives death ... physical death in this life and eternal separation from God in the lake of fire in eternity.

God's justice demands payment for sin ... but God's love wants to provide pardon, peace, and eternal life. God's solution to the dilemma was to send His perfect Son to earth to die in our place. When Jesus was on the cross He received the punishment for sin we deserved. "But he was pierced for our transgressions, he was crushed for our iniquities; the punishment that brought us peace was upon him, and by his wounds we are healed. We all, like sheep, have gone astray, each of us has turned to his own way; and the Lord has laid on him the iniquity of us all" (Isaiah 53:5–6).

Was God's plan successful? Yes! The resurrection of Jesus from the dead was proof that His sacrifice was sufficient payment for our sin. "And if Christ has not been raised, your faith is futile; you are still in your sins. . . . But Christ has indeed been raised from the dead" (1 Corinthians 15:17, 20). When Jesus exploded from the tomb on that first Easter morning, He shattered death's hold on humanity and demonstrated His victory over sin and death.

Do you believe you have sinned against God? Do you believe Jesus Christ is God's Son and that He died on the cross to pay the penalty for your sins? Do you believe He rose from the dead? If so, are you willing to accept His payment for your sin and trust in Him for your eternal destiny? This is the starting place for your journey of faith. God does not require you to accomplish great deeds, make great sacrifices, or experience great suffering to gain eternal life. Jesus alone has done it all. You need to believe His actions are sufficient . . . and place your life in His hands. If you have never done so, perhaps you could pray a prayer like the following:

Dear Lord, I know I have done wrong and fallen short of Your perfect ways. I also know and believe You sent Your Son, Jesus Christ, to earth to die on the cross to pay the penalty for my sin. I now want to place my trust in Jesus Christ as the substitute for my sin. Please forgive me and give me eternal life. In Christ's name I ask this. Amen.

If you just prayed this prayer in sincerity, congratulations! You are now part of the family of God. How can you be sure? Because God said so in His Word. "And this is the testimony:

God has given us eternal life, and this life is in his Son. He who has the Son has life; he who does not have the Son of God does not have life. I write these things to you who believe in the name of the Son of God so that you may know that you have eternal life" (1 John 5:11–13).

If you have placed your trust in Jesus Christ as your personal Savior, what's next? Having trusted in Christ for our eternal destiny, we must now learn to trust Him for our day-to-day needs. Abraham can be our example. His life of faith involved following God's directions, believing God's words, and obeying God's commands. You can do the same.

Reflect and Respond

Faith is more than just intellectual assent, more than just believing a set of facts. It's an active trust in God and His Word.

1. Have you placed your trust for eternal life in Jesus Christ and His death on your behalf? If you just made this decision, find a church that believes and teaches the Bible . . . and tell the pastor what you have done.
2. In what areas do you struggle most to trust God?
3. Make a list of the specific ways you have seen God work in your life. Keep the list nearby and read through it whenever you struggle with doubt. Remembering what He has done for you in the past will help you trust Him for the future.
4. Memorize Hebrew 11:1 and ask God to help you grow stronger in your faith.

"And without faith it is impossible to please God, because anyone who comes to him must believe that he exists and

that he rewards those who earnestly seek him."
(Hebrews 11:6)

THE LORD DOESN'T ASK ABOUT YOUR
ABILITY, ONLY YOUR AVAILABILITY; AND,
IF YOU PROVE YOUR DEPENDABILITY,
THE LORD WILL INCREASE YOUR
CAPABILITY.

—*Unknown*

6

CAN GOD DEPEND ON ME?:
Faithfulness

Dependability sells! Four decades ago Timex sold watches on live national television by focusing on dependability. The announcer would do something outrageous like strap the watch to the propeller of an outboard motor and run the engine in a tank of water. He would then stop the engine, remove the watch, and hold it up for the camera. As the audience looked at the second hand sweep around the dial, the announcer delivered the punch line. "Timex! Takes a lickin' and keeps on tickin'!" In those unpredictable days of early television, this stunt spoke volumes about the faith the company had in the watch's dependability. "Buy me," the advertisement screamed. "I won't let you down."

Dependability still sells. The lonely Maytag repairman, with his clean uniform and sad expression reinforces the message that Maytag is produced by "the dependability people." Your Maytag appliance won't let you down!

But the darling of dependability in advertising today has to be the ubiquitous Energizer bunny. It keeps going, and going, and going . . . . outpacing marathoners and outlasting everyone from Darth Vader to Santa Claus. With every beat of the drum this fuzzy pink rabbit reminds viewers that his batteries last longer. Your Energizer batteries won't let you down.

If only life matched the ads!

THE CAR FROM SPUTTER CITY

I can recall in vivid detail the first "new" car my wife, Kathy, and I bought. Actually, it wasn't really new. It was a dealer demonstrator, but the odometer read less than 12,000 miles when we bought it. It looked great! Before buying the car we watched television ads that stressed its innovative features and solid construction. I'll not share the name of the manufacturer . . . but I will tell you about "the car from sputter city"!

I began having my doubts about the car when the hood, trunk, and roof started turning a lighter shade of red than the doors and fenders. The car developed the automotive equivalent of "male pattern baldness." But the real crisis began during rush hour in Harrisburg, Pennsylvania, in the middle of a blizzard.

I had driven to Pennsylvania to attend a funeral. On my way home the car just stopped in the middle of downtown Harrisburg. Died! Quit! Conked out! Sleet mixed with snow pelted my face as I pulled off the road and looked under the hood. Everything looked okay, so I climbed back in the car and left the hood up, waiting for a policeman to come by to rescue me. Out of frustration I turned the key one last time. The motor sprang to life as if nothing was wrong! And so the problems began.

Over the next year the car took on a mind of its own. Day or night. Wet or dry. Summer or winter. Cold or hot. Superhighway or country road. In no predictable pattern and for no detectable reason the car would just stop running.

I know what you're thinking. "Why didn't you take the car to a dealership to have it fixed?" We did. Many times. They changed the computer module . . . twice! We discovered a recall for a part in the engine and had it replaced. No difference. One problem was that the car would never act up at the dealership.

Once we were driving to a store when the car began to sputter. We were only a few miles from the dealership so I did a quick U-turn and headed that direction. Now they would *have* to find the problem. But the closer I got to the dealership the less the car shook. With the garage in sight the last bit of hesitation disappeared and the car purred smoothly. Rats! Finally I couldn't take it anymore. I'm not a skilled mechanic (today's politically correct society would classify me as mechanically challenged), but even I could tell the problem was electrical. The solution? Replace every electrical part possible. So, armed with boxes of replacement parts, I attacked the problem. In two of the boxes I found a small notice saying the new part may not look like the original because it had been modified to correct a potential problem. Aha!

After many trips to the dealership, hundreds of dollars in "expert" repairs, and countless hours sitting beside the road waiting for the car to restart, I finally solved the problem. Two defective parts allowed moisture to collect and, temporarily, disrupt, the electrical system. We sold that car a few months later, and we have never owned another car made by that company.

Dependability is important.

HOW IMPORTANT IS FAITHFULNESS?

We value faithfulness and dependability as ideals, but sadly we don't really expect to find them. Fact is, we are often surprised when we do. In the past, manufacturers sought to develop "brand loyalty" among their customers . . . loyalty that passed from generation to generation. "My father drove a Plymouth. I drive a Plymouth. And my son will drive a Plymouth." But brand loyalty has gone the way of the Nash, Hudson, Henry J, Studebaker, Oldsmobile . . . and now Pontiac. Today we change brands almost as often as we change clothes.

Why? Some of the reason has to do with dependability— if it's no longer dependable, why should we bother?

Brand loyalty is a two-way street. Many manufacturers cut corners and cheapen products to save money. At the same time they inflate claims in their advertising and pitch products that can never meet the expectations they create. After spending tens of thousands of dollars to purchase "precision driving machines," customers fume countless hours in dealership waiting rooms while their cars have parts replaced in a recall. It's hard to remain loyal to a particular brand or company when you feel ripped off.

A lack of brand loyalty in the marketplace might be a sign of healthy competition and free market economics, but the same attitude has crept into our homes and families. And there it produces misery, anger, and pain. We have replaced "Till death do us part" with prenuptial agreements, and we hardly raise an eyebrow when we hear about someone having an affair. Today divorce is no big deal. Incompatibility. Irreconcilable differences. No-fault divorce. For some, marriage is no larger a commitment than going on a date or picking out a puppy. You hope it will work out, but if it doesn't . . .

The church fares little better than the home. God ordained the local church to be a gathering of the faithful. Members of a local congregation are to be the visible representation of God's light to their community. Yet today, many Christians shop for churches like they shop for cars. Which is the most stylish? The biggest? The one with the most features? The most powerful? People "test drive" the worship service and see what other "options" the church has to offer.

> MANY LIVE LIVES OF FAITHFUL OBSCURITY . . . THEIR RELIABILITY TAKEN FOR GRANTED. OTHERS HAVE DEMONSTRATED FAITHFULNESS WHILE IN THE PUBLIC EYE.

People look for a church where their needs can be met—though that isn't necessarily a bad thing—more than where they can worship and be of service to others. Churches must "market" themselves to attract and hold potential "customers." But churches that always cater to what the "customers" *want* to hear, seldom can afford to share with those people the message they desperately *need* to hear.

Faithfulness. Dependability. Trustworthiness. Everyone values it, but few practice it consistently. Yet models of faithfulness *do* exist. Many live lives of faithful obscurity . . . their reliability taken for granted. Others have demonstrated faithfulness while in the public eye. Billy Graham, for example, has always been one of my personal heroes. He's given a lifetime of service without a hint of financial or sexual impropriety.

Another hero of mine is Chuck Swindoll. Gifted speaker. Talented writer. Fun-loving, Harley-riding leader. But more than all that, he is a man of faithfulness. Faithfulness to God. Faithfulness to Cynthia and his children. Faithfulness to the ministries he leads. Faithfulness to those who work beside him in ministry. And I had that privilege at Dallas Seminary.

During the years I served with Chuck I once had to fly back to Pennsylvania for a family emergency. My dad was scheduled to undergo heart bypass surgery. I know bypass surgery is quite common. It's almost considered routine. All those things are true unless it's *your* father being wheeled to surgery on the gurney.

I went to be with Mom during the operation. The hours dragged by as we waited for the doctor to tell us how the operation had gone. Even after Dad came out of surgery we spent several more days waiting for those precious few moments each hour when we could enter the cardiac care unit to be with him.

During one visitation period in the cardiac care unit the nurse called me aside and said my physician from Dallas had called to check on Dad's progress. My physician from Dallas? "Yes," she said, "Dr. Swindoll!" What a guy!

Dad recovered, and I flew back to Dallas. On my desk was a handwritten note from Chuck that read, in part, "You have been through a long and lonely journey these past several days. I understand. I've been there with my dad. So many, many times you have come to my mind. Each time I've sent a word upward. . . . What a great feeling is relief! With a smile that says 'Welcome back.'" I treasure that note, and I deeply appreciated Chuck's faithfulness in writing it.

So how can we become more faithful? What can the Bible offer to help us develop lives characterized by faithfulness? Two hardened military veterans, Joshua and Caleb, can supply us with some answers.

Hangin' with Moses

Faithfulness begins in small areas. Joshua stepped onto the pages of Bible history to lead a party of warriors against a group of nomadic raiders. These nomads, the Amalekites, attacked the Israelites in the wilderness. They needed to be stopped, and Moses put Joshua in charge of the commandos.

Though the whole account of the battle takes only nine verses (Exodus 17:8–16), the Bible makes two crucial observations about Joshua. First, he faithfully executed Moses's orders. "So Joshua fought the Amalekites *as Moses had ordered* [italics added]." Why add this phrase? Perhaps to set Joshua apart from the rest of the people. Just a few verses earlier the people "quarreled with Moses" and "grumbled against Moses" (Exodus 17:2–3). Second, Joshua completed the assignment. "So Joshua overcame the Amalekite army with the sword" (17:13). The children of Israel were whiners, Joshua was a winner.

Moses found in Joshua someone he could trust to obey

orders and to follow the job through to completion. The battle was over in just one day—the entire encounter nothing more than a brief footnote in the amazing events that took place during those forty years in the wilderness. Yet Joshua's faithfulness this one day changed his life forever. The next time Joshua appears in the Bible he has received a promotion. "Then Moses set out with Joshua his aide" (Exodus 24:13). Moses made Joshua his assistant. When Moses went up Mount Sinai to meet with God, Joshua walked beside. What a promotion!

What responsibilities do you have today? How faithful have you been? No job should be too small or insignificant. "Serve wholeheartedly, as if you were serving the Lord, not men, because you know that the Lord will reward everyone for whatever good he does" (Ephesians 6:7–8).

The Mossad's First Mission

The Mossad is modern Israel's crack intelligence organization—Israel's version of America's CIA. This group of supersleuths has tracked down escaped Nazis and political terrorists. They have also pulled off some of the most dangerous and daring undercover operations in history . . . and we only know a fraction of the things they have done!

Even today's Mossad would be proud of their nation's first spy mission—undertaken over 3,400 years before the modern state of Israel came into existence. The children of Israel stood on the edge of the land promised them by God. But this new nation knew little about the land they were about to invade. Moses chose twelve spies to explore the new land, and he issued specific instructions (Numbers 13):

- "See what the land is like and whether the people who live there are strong or weak, few or many." (Check out the opposition.)

- "What kind of land do they live in? Is it good or bad?"
  (Check out the terrain.)
- "What kind of towns do they live in? Are they
  unwalled or fortified?"
  (Check out the defenses.)
- "How is the soil? Is it fertile or poor?"
  (Check out the potential.)
- "Are there trees on it or not?"
  (Check out the productivity.)

And whom did Moses select for this elite group of spies?
"From the tribe of Ephraim, Hoshea son of Nun" (Numbers
13:8). What? Who's "Hoshea"? I thought you were talking
about Joshua? Be patient! Moses explains who this is a few
verses later. "Moses gave Hoshea son of Nun the name Joshua"
(Numbers 13:16). Evidently, Joshua's original name was
Hoshea ("salvation"). Moses changed it (possibly after the victory over the Amalekites) to Joshua ("the Lord saves"). The
Bible provides the names of all twelve spies, but only one is
singled out in this fashion. Joshua is the spy with the new
name . . . a name that focuses attention on the Lord.

The spies returned with their report. All agreed the land
was fertile and productive. "It does flow with milk and honey!
Here is its fruit" (Numbers 13:27). But the spies could not
agree on their evaluation of the people of the land. Ten of the
spies issued a majority report . . . and it wasn't good news.

- "The people who live there are powerful."
  (They are too strong.)
- "The cities are fortified and very large."
  (They are too well defended.)
- "We even saw descendants of Anak [i.e., giants] there."
  (They are too big!)

To slaves wandering through the desert, walls of stone and brick must have appeared almost insurmountable. The army of Egypt had experience attacking fortified cities, but to these simple peasants the task looked hopeless. And to most of the ragtag band of spies the locals looked physically larger and more powerful.

Two spies—Joshua and Caleb—stood and challenged the majority report. They didn't see obstacles, they saw opportunities. Caleb spoke first, "We should go up and take possession of the land, for we can certainly do it" (Numbers 13:30). When the people refused to listen, both Joshua and Caleb stressed the wonderful opportunity being rejected. "The land we passed through and explored is exceedingly good" (Numbers 14:7). How could these two see the land and people so differently than the other ten spies?

Joshua's and Caleb's method was their ability to view all possible problems from God's perspective.

> **Problem #1:** This "good land" is populated by powerful people, some of whom are giants.
> **Answer:** "And do not be afraid of the people of the land, because we will swallow them up" (Numbers 14:9).
> I like the poetic nature of the King James translation here. "They are bread for us." We'll eat 'em up!
> **Problem #2:** These powerful people live in large, fortified cities.
> **Answer:** "Their protection is gone, but the Lord is with us" (Numbers 14:9).

Joshua and Caleb did not walk through Canaan wearing rose-colored glasses. They saw the same problems, but they saw them through God's eyes. Physical giants are no threat when God is on our side. High walls and thick gates are no barrier when God removes their protection. The real threat to Israel was not the people of Canaan or their defenses. The most serious threat was the temptation to abandon God. Joshua and Caleb started and ended their speech in Numbers 14:9 with a warning. "Only do not rebel against the Lord. . . . Do not be afraid of them [the Canaanites]."

The final vote wasn't even close. When the 603,550 men of fighting age made their decision on which report to accept, Joshua and Caleb lost in a landslide—603,548 voted for the majority report! In fact, the "whole assembly talked about stoning them" (Numbers 14:10). Joshua and Caleb had *no* support from anyone else. Peer pressure is something all of us have faced at some point. We all know how difficult it is to appear to "stand out" in a crowd. Imagine the pressure on Joshua and Caleb! No one from their tribes . . . or clans . . . or families stood with them. How were they able to do it?

CALEB'S DOGGED DETERMINATION

"Caleb" in Hebrew means "dog," and Caleb certainly had the tenacity of a bulldog. He shared his secret for faithfulness when he appeared before Joshua after the forty-year period of wandering in the wilderness to ask for his inheritance in the land. What kept Caleb faithful? Conviction, commitment, and confidence.

Conviction

Caleb could stand alone with Joshua because Moses had asked for a truthful appraisal, "And I brought him back a report according to my convictions" (Joshua 14:7). He could stand alone because he knew what he was standing for. He had a deep, abiding belief in what he knew to be true, and he was willing to take a stand for what was right.

Commitment

Knowing the truth of what you believe is one thing. Being willing to stand by those beliefs is another. Caleb saw the tide turn against his convictions. The crowd didn't buy his arguments. Wasn't this the time for compromise . . . acquiescence . . . reconsideration? Not for Caleb! "I, however, followed the Lord my God wholeheartedly" (Joshua 14:8). If God was bigger than the giants in the land, He was also bigger than the disbelieving Israelites in the wilderness. Caleb cast his lot with God.

Confidence

Faithfulness is a by-product of faith. (See the previous chapter.) I can be faithful to God if I'm absolutely sure He will do what He has promised. Caleb was faithful because He had complete confidence in God . . . and that confidence came from experience. God promised Joshua and Caleb he would keep them alive in the wilderness and allow them to enter the Promised Land. Forty years of wandering in the wilderness was followed by five years of active warfare as Israel fought to take the land. So what became of God's promise? "Now then, just as the Lord promised, he has kept me alive for forty-five years since the time he said this to Moses . . . So here I am today, eighty-five years old! I am still as strong today as the day Moses sent me out; I'm just as vigorous to go out to battle now as I was then" (Joshua 14:10–11).

Caleb's confidence came from watching God work. The

> JOSHUA WAS PREPARED TO CONQUER THE PHYSICAL GIANTS IN THE LAND, BUT HOW COULD HE HOPE TO REPLACE A SPIRITUAL GIANT LIKE MOSES?

God who had helped him in the past could be trusted for the future. He was so confident he went to Joshua with a bold request. "Now give me this hill country that the Lord promised me that day. You yourself heard then that the Anakites [the giants!] were there and their cities were large and fortified, but, the Lord helping me, I will drive them out just as he said" (Joshua 14:12). At the age of eighty-five Caleb wasn't ready to retire. He wanted a piece of the action. And he didn't want anything too easy. He wanted the hills with the largest giants and the strongest cities! God hadn't changed, and Caleb was as confident of the outcome now as he had been forty-five years earlier!

COMMANDER AND CHIEF

Turning back to Joshua for a moment, we find him facing the greatest challenge of his life. For forty years Joshua served as second-in-command to Moses. Great guy—wonderful commander—fabulous assistant! But could he replace Moses? I'm sure some in Israel had their doubts. It's hard following a legend like Moses who led so powerfully for so long. The book of Deuteronomy ends with a suitable epitaph that captures the essence of Moses's leadership. "For no one has ever shown the mighty power or performed the awesome deeds that Moses did in the sight of all Israel" (Deuteronomy 34:12). Joshua was prepared to conquer the physical giants in the land, but how could he hope to replace a spiritual giant like Moses?

God appeared to Joshua with the answer. Three times He urged Joshua to "be strong and courageous" (Joshua 1:6, 7, 9). Joshua, like Caleb, had to develop conviction, commitment, and confidence. Each element was as essential for Joshua's faithfulness as it was for Caleb's.

Conviction

Joshua had to be convinced he was God's choice to lead Israel. Though he did not possess the unique personality of Moses, he had to realize God would supply the needed ability to lead. "Now Joshua son of Nun was filled with the spirit of wisdom because Moses had laid his hands on him" (Deuteronomy 34:9). Spiritual leadership is dependent on God's spiritual enablement, not on natural ability. Israel needed Moses in the wilderness, but they needed Joshua for the conquest. God wanted to convince Joshua of this, so He said, "Be strong and courageous, because you will lead these people to inherit the land." Joshua was God's choice.

Commitment

Conviction alone wasn't enough to guarantee faithfulness. Conviction had to be followed by personal commitment. God reminded Joshua of his need to know and obey the Word of God. God would measure Joshua's success as a leader by his commitment to His Word. "Be strong and very courageous. Be careful to obey all the law my servant Moses gave you; *do not turn from it to the right or to the left*, that you may be successful wherever you go. Do not let this Book of the Law depart from your mouth; meditate on it day and night, so that you may be careful to do everything written in it. Then you will be prosperous and successful [italics added]" (Joshua 1:7–8).

Joshua may personally have felt inadequate as a leader, but he had to develop the conviction that God called him to replace Moses. God would give him the ability to be an effective leader, but those convictions called for commitment. To be an effective leader Joshua needed to master the ability to submit to the heavenly King and wholeheartedly obey Him.

A few chapters later God reminded Joshua of the necessity of this commitment. Just after crossing the Jordan River, Joshua prepared to begin his conquest of the land. Jericho loomed as the first major obstacle. Camped just a few miles from this walled fortress, Joshua felt the full weight of his position as commander-in-chief. What if the city proved too difficult to conquer? What if the people of the land were better warriors? What if the toll in human life proved to be too great?

Whatever Joshua was thinking, his thoughts were interrupted by a man standing in front of him with a drawn sword. Joshua didn't recognize him so he asked, "Are you for us or for our enemies?" (Joshua 5:13). The warrior's answer startled him. "'Neither,' he replied, 'but as commander of the army of the Lord I have now come'" (Joshua 5:14). God had not promised unswerving allegiance to Israel, He had called on Israel to promise unswerving allegiance to *Him.* God's heavenly forces could fight for Israel—or against Israel.

God's commander was in Israel's midst watching for signs of obedience and commitment. Joshua immediately fell face down and humbly asked this heavenly Commander, "What message does my Lord have for his servant?" The burdens and problems of leadership now came into proper focus. The battle belonged to God, not Joshua. God was in charge, and Joshua was to be the committed servant.

But Joshua still needed one final element to help him develop faithfulness—an absolute sense of confidence that would take him through the battles ahead.

Confidence

God often tests commitment in the crucible of conflict. It's easy to commit to God when manna shows up on the ground each morning and God is appearing to you in visions. It's harder to have confidence when the wheels come off and God seems to be silent. Joshua had to gear himself up for the hard times ahead. God's solution was to reaffirm His protection.

"Be strong and courageous. Do not be terrified; do not be discouraged, for the Lord your God will be with you wherever you go" (Joshua 1:9).

Did Joshua remain confident? At Jericho Joshua ordered the people, "Shout! For the Lord has given you the city!" (Joshua 6:16). The outcome was never in doubt. Joshua led Israel in victorious conquest because he *knew* God would give victory. Later Joshua ordered the heavens to halt their movement on Israel's behalf. "Joshua said to the Lord in the presence of Israel: 'O sun, stand still over Gibeon, O moon, over the Valley of Aijalon'" (Joshua 10:12). That's confidence! He knew God would do what He had promised.

AS FOR ME AND MY HOUSE

Society idolizes the strength and beauty of youth, but true wisdom belongs to those who have mastered life and its secrets. The next generation of Israelite leaders were busy developing their new land when they received a summons to appear at Shechem. Over twenty years had passed since Joshua had led Israel in conquest and divided the land among the tribes. Joshua, the seasoned sage, was summoning Israel's new leaders for one final meeting before his impending death. What final words of wisdom would this battle-hardened veteran give to the next generation?

It's no surprise that the man whose life epitomized faithful service for God focused on the subject of faithfulness. After reviewing all God had done for the nation, Joshua called the leaders to action. "Now fear the Lord and serve him with all faithfulness" (Joshua 24:14). This elder statesman had no illusions about the temptations facing the fledgling nation. He had lived long enough to see an entire generation reject the Lord and perish in the wilderness. He watched good soldiers die because of one man's sin at Jericho. The temptation to turn from the Lord was great, and the consequences could be catastrophic.

Joshua laid the issue on the line with this gathering of leaders. "But if serving the Lord seems undesirable to you, then choose for yourselves this day whom you will serve . . . But as for me and my household, we will serve the Lord" (Joshua 24:15). Joshua planned to end his life the way he had always lived it . . . in faithful service to God. And he challenged the next generation to tread the same path.

Joshua and Caleb. Two men from different family backgrounds—one from the tribe of Ephraim, the other from the rival tribe of Judah. Men who assumed different levels of responsibility during Israel's wanderings in the wilderness and during the conquest of Canaan. Yet two men who shared the same characteristic of unswerving faithfulness to their God . . . whose lives ran counter to an entire generation.

In the great celestial arena Joshua and Caleb must surely have box seats to watch today's race of the faithful. They must be part of the "great cloud of witnesses" that surround us as we "run with perseverance the race marked out for us" (Hebrews 12:1). They are cheering us on with their own testimonies of faithfulness to God. And they are pointing to the supreme example of faithfulness . . . Jesus Christ. "Consider him who endured such opposition from sinful men, so that you will not grow weary and lose heart" (Hebrews 12:3).

Caleb and Joshua faithfully followed God even when it required them to stand against the rest of the nation. And now God asks you to make the same commitment. Are you ready, and willing, to repeat after Joshua, "Choose for yourselves this day whom you will serve . . . . But as for me and my household, we will serve the Lord" (Joshua 24:15)? Why not make that commitment right now?

Reflect and Respond

Faithfulness is our commitment to remain true to God whatever the circumstances. Several elements characterize an individual who is faithful.

1. Faithfulness begins with strong convictions. Do you know what you believe, based on the teaching of God's Word? Do you attend a local church, Sunday school class, or Bible study where you are able to learn what God's Word really says?
2. Faithfulness follows commitment. Are you willing to commit to follow God and obey Him? Write out your commitment on a piece of paper and put it in your Bible as a reminder. Or better yet, write your commitment in your Bible, sign it, and date it. This can be your physical reminder . . . your "large stone" (Joshua 24:26) set up to keep you from forgetting your commitment to follow God.
3. If someone were writing about your life, what would they say about your conviction, commitment, confidence?
4. Faithfulness allows us to stay true to God because we maintain confidence in Him. Make a list of the ways God has met your physical, spiritual, and emotional needs over the past year. Be specific. Keep a prayer journal to chronicle the ways God has been working in your life.
5. Memorize Joshua 24:15 and ask God to help make those words the passion of your life.

"Let love and faithfulness never leave you; bind them around your neck, write them on the tablet of your heart. Then you will win favor and a good name in the sight of God and man." (Proverbs 3:3–4)

AIM AT HEAVEN AND YOU WILL GET
EARTH THROWN IN. AIM AT EARTH AND
YOU GET NEITHER.

—*C. S. Lewis*

ONE CAN GIVE WITHOUT LOVING, BUT
ONE CANNOT LOVE WITHOUT GIVING.

—*Amy Carmichael*

7

PASTRIES AND PERFUME:
Balance

OUT OF BALANCE

once worked in the banking business. No, I didn't work for any of the banks that collapsed . . . nor did I ever receive a multimillion dollar bonus. (I never received *any* bonus!) To help pay for my graduate studies I worked part-time as a teller at the drive-in window of a small local bank. They needed part-time help, and as a graduate student I needed a job.

Every weekday (except holidays) I sat at my window overseeing two drive-though lanes. Most afternoons were predictable. But I dreaded Fridays as well as both the fifteenth and final days of each month. Those were the high-volume days when lines of cars would stretch back to the street. And if the fifteenth or the final day of the month fell *on* Friday, the workers cashing paychecks, stores making deposits, and individuals getting money for the weekend overwhelmed us.

The most stressful moment of all on those days came when we closed the bank and "balanced out" for the day. The process seemed simple enough. Start with the opening balance in my cash drawer. Add the slips for cash deposits. Subtract the checks and slips for cash withdrawals . . . and pray to God the closing balance matched the actual amount of money remaining! If the drawer was "out of balance," I was forced to go back and check every transaction to see if the slips matched each cash deposit and withdrawal. A laborious, but necessary, process.

Balance benefits more than bank tellers. It's essential for living life successfully. Balance is the ability to hold everything in harmony . . . to keep differing elements in a state of equilibrium. We don't think much about balance until something goes wrong that throws our lives into disarray.

- While reconciling your checkbook with your monthly bank statement you realize you forgot to enter a check for $150 . . . and your checkbook has been *out of balance.*
- You begin an exercise program but develop severe cramping while working out. A blood test shows a chemical *imbalance* . . . a potassium deficiency . . . is causing the cramping.
- Your car steering wheel shakes and vibrates as you drive. A mechanic identifies the problem . . . your tires are *out of balance.*
- You awaken in the morning. But as you stand up, waves of dizziness and nausea overwhelm you, forcing you back into bed. You call your doctor who suspects an inner ear infection that is throwing off your *sense of balance.*

Living a life of integrity requires balance. Solomon, the wise king who unfortunately lived much of his life out of balance, concluded in the end: "There is a time for everything, and a season for every activity under heaven" (Ecclesiastes 3:1). The difficulty is discovering God's balance.

Without a sense of balance some Christians *burn out* from overactivity while others *rust out* from lack of involvement. Still others *foul out* from wrong decisions and bad choices. In any case . . . you're out! Jesus recognized—and taught—the importance of balance.

On one particular occasion Jesus sent the twelve disciples on a vital mission throughout Israel (Mark 6:7–13). They preached, cast out demons, and performed miraculous healings. When they came back to Jesus, they were wild with success, brimming over with enthusiasm. Crowds followed them back to the Master! Pandemonium prevailed as the masses packed ever more closely around Jesus and His disciples. Jesus and the disciples "did not even have a chance to eat" (6:31). Men and women were pressing in from all sides, hoping to see—or experience—these miracle workers in action. It was an exciting and exhausting time.

And then Jesus said, "Come with me by yourselves to a quiet place and get some rest" (Mark 6:31). I picture the disciples almost shaking their heads in disbelief. "What! Leave when the excitement is just beginning to build? The discipleship business is booming! Sure we're hungry, but we can't stop now!" They were preoccupied with ministry, but they needed a lesson in balance. Too much busyness . . . even when it's busyness on behalf of God . . . can be harmful.

What is the key for maintaining balance? How can we keep our lives from spinning out of control? Perhaps we can find some answers in a home Jesus visited numerous times . . . the home of Mary, Martha, and Lazarus in the village of Bethany. We are invited into their home on three separate occasions in the Bible. And each visit is instructive.

ALMOST MISSING TIME WITH GOD

As Jesus and His disciples traveled through Israel they relied on friends and followers to supply food and lodging. Ordinary individuals opened their homes to show hospitality to the Son of God. Most remain anonymous, but one special family is identified by name. Perhaps it's because their location near Jerusalem made their home a particular favorite. Perhaps it's because of the close-knit bond that developed between the two sisters, their brother, and the Lord. Or perhaps it's because of the unique events that took place inside the walls of their house. But for whatever reason, the home of Mary, Martha, and Lazarus took on special significance in the life of our Lord.

The village of Bethany sits on the eastern slope of the Mount of Olives. Though Jews from the northern part of the country could travel directly south from Galilee to Jerusalem through Samaria, many chose to bypass that region—adding an additional two or three days to their journey—because of the animosity between the Jews and the Samaritans. These Jews took a more roundabout road to Jerusalem that led them down the eastern side of the Jordan Valley toward the Dead Sea. The travelers would then cross the Jordan near Jericho and make the long, winding journey up from Jericho to Jerusalem. After a steep climb through the Judean Wilderness, the Mount of Olives would rise up as the last obstacle to Jerusalem. Bethany sat just below the brow of the hill on its eastern side, a mere two miles from Jerusalem. The village made a logical resting place after the daylong journey from Jericho.

Jesus and His disciples used both roadways to travel to and from Jerusalem. On one occasion Jesus "had to go through Samaria" because of a divine appointment with a woman at a well (John 4:4). But on other occasions Jesus traveled through Jericho on His way to Jerusalem (see Matthew 20:29). His friends and followers who lived along the different roads had no way of knowing when—or if—Jesus and His disciples might stop to seek lodging.

The gospel of Luke presents every hostess's nightmare. Friends dropping by without notice. Unexpected. . . but not unwelcome! "As Jesus and his disciples were on their way, he came to a village where a woman named Martha opened her home to him" (Luke 10:38).

Picture the scene. No sooner had Jesus and the disciples walked through the door than Martha sprang into action. Someone needs to go to the cistern to draw more water to wash their feet. But what about the evening meal? Extra grain must be ground for bread. Wait! Before grinding the grain, I'll need still more water to prepare the dough. Stop! Before I prepare the dough, the fire should be burning in the oven. Oh no! We're almost out of firewood. Someone needs to collect extra firewood before we start the fire. Hold it! We don't have enough fruit or vegetables to feed all the guests. Someone needs to go to the market to buy the necessary produce.

Martha's mind went into overdrive. "But Martha was distracted by all the preparations that had to be made" (Luke 10:40). Don't judge Martha too harshly. Hospitality was an important part of ancient Near Eastern culture, and Martha was serving Israel's Messiah. My wife sometimes reminds me that if it weren't for the Marthas of the world nothing would ever get done. Martha, the conscientious host, was responsible for running the household, and she took her job seriously.

> MARY REMAINED PLANTED AT THE LORD'S FEET, HER EYES GLUED TO HIS FACE.

But Martha was not the only woman in the house. She had a younger sister, Mary. While Martha ran around drawing water, washing, grinding, kneading, baking, peeling. Mary "sat at the Lord's feet listening to what he said" (Luke 10:39). Oblivious to the whirlwind of activity taking place around her, Mary sat quietly, soaking in the words of her Lord.

I suspect Martha first tried some "subtle" ways to get Mary's attention. A few glares in Mary's direction. A few clicks of her tongue to her teeth. Some clearing of her throat . . . loudly! Perhaps she carried a pot of water just a little too conspicuously through the room on her way back from the cistern, pausing just long enough to sigh aloud. But it was all in vain. Mary remained planted at the Lord's feet, her eyes glued to His face. She listened so intently to the Lord she never noticed her sister's preparations, or her rising level of frustration.

Martha finally chose a more direct course of action. If Mary listened so intently to Jesus, then Martha would get Jesus to set her straight. And besides, Jesus should have noticed Mary wasn't acting as a proper hostess. So Martha marched up to Jesus and said, "Lord, don't you care that my sister has left me to do the work by myself? Tell her to help me!" (Luke 10:40). Bam! Martha had the subtlety of a two-by-four.

Jesus' gentle response certainly raised some eyebrows in a society that expected men to sit around and discuss "weighty issues" while women did housework. "'Martha, Martha,' the Lord answered, 'you are worried and upset about many things, but only one thing is needed. Mary has chosen what is better, and it will not be taken away from her'" (Luke 10:41–42). Martha was so "worried and upset" about the details that she missed the big picture. Jesus was in her house teaching . . . and she was too busy counting cups to pay attention.

> OUR SOCIETY FOSTERS THE "MARTHA SYNDROME." WE REWARD DILIGENCE AND APPLAUD ACTIVITY.

Unfortunately, we often miss the point of this story. Our response goes something like this: Boy! If Jesus ever came to my house, I wouldn't worry about fixing dinner. I'd call Domino's or Little Caesars and sit at His feet till the pizza arrived! But Jesus had more in mind than dinner.

Everything Martha was doing was good and proper. Her problem was that she focused so much on these details that she lost her perspective. She wanted to prepare a feast when a simple meal would have sufficed. She worried about drawing water from the cistern while the fountain of living water sat in the next room. She fretted over preparing enough bread while the bread of life lodged in her house. She concentrated on the trees . . . and missed the forest.

Our society fosters the "Martha syndrome." We reward diligence and applaud activity. We crave "labor-saving devices" to give us more free time. But we use those devices to cram more activity into the same twenty-four-hour period. Our news comes from RSS feeds on our computer rather than the newspaper or television. Our cell phones must have Internet access. And texting has replaced e-mail for many because it's more immediate. In the midst of all this activity, like Martha, we become "worried and upset about many things."

Are you too busy to pray and read your Bible? How much time do you take each day to sit at the Lord's feet? Ouch! For many of us, it seems easier to live life as Martha rather than Mary. We have so much to do, so many projects to accomplish. It's just hard to find time to spend with Jesus. But a life in balance will carve out time with the Lord.

ALMOST MISSING WHAT GOD IS DOING

If someone were to set to music Jesus' visits to the home of Mary and Martha, the second visit would begin in a minor key. In the first visit Luke focused on the two sisters, but as the apostle John reports the second visit he reveals they had a brother, Lazarus. In John 11 we join Jesus and His disciples as a messenger arrives from Bethany with an urgent request from Mary and Martha.

Jesus was staying "across the Jordan . . . where John had been baptizing in the early days" (John 10:40). The messenger had traveled from Bethany to Jericho, forded the Jordan River—probably by small boat—and journeyed several more miles to another Bethany ("beyond the Jordan") where he heard Jesus might be ministering. Two towns named Bethany, barely twenty miles apart, each visited by Jesus on multiple occasions. Yet for Mary and Martha the other Bethany might as well have been on the other side of the Roman Empire, because it was too far away to summon Jesus in time to save Lazarus.

After traveling all day the messenger found Jesus and delivered his heartfelt plea from the two sisters. "Lord, the one you love is sick" (John 11:3). Lazarus was dying, and these faithful sisters needed a miracle from God's Messiah to save him. Unfortunately, Lazarus probably died shortly after the messenger left Bethany. It took about one day to travel from Bethany through the rugged Judean Wilderness to the region east of Jericho, and at least one day to return back to Bethany. Before making the journey to Bethany Jesus "stayed where he was two more days" (John 11:6)—making a total of at least four days from the time the messenger left Bethany until Jesus arrived. And on His arrival Jesus was told that Lazarus "had already been in the tomb for four days" (John 11:17).

Imagine the grief of Mary and Martha. Once they realized how ill their brother was, they sent for the one person who could heal him. They knew from reports where Jesus was ministering. As Lazarus's condition deteriorated they knew the messenger might not reach Jesus in time. And yet, they must have hoped against hope that Jesus had somehow sensed their need and had already started toward Bethany. Glancing from Lazarus . . . to the door . . . then back to Lazarus, they desperately prayed that Jesus would arrive just in time to heal their brother. But the door never opened . . . Jesus didn't come . . . and Lazarus died before the day ended.

The mind-numbing suddenness of Lazarus's death and burial struck Mary and Martha with the force of a Roman battering ram. They quickly prepared his body for burial and put it in the family tomb before sundown. The family must have laid Lazarus to rest just about the time the messenger reached Jesus with the news of his illness.

Late the next day the messenger returned with still more disturbing news. Yes, he had found Jesus and delivered the message. No, Jesus was not following just behind. Jesus had seemed remarkably calm on hearing the news. After announcing, "This sickness will not end in death" (John 11:4), Jesus decided to stay where He was for a few more days. No, Jesus did not say when . . . or if . . . He would come to Bethany.

Two additional days pass in a blur of grief and bewilderment. Why hadn't Jesus come? How could He have been so wrong about Lazarus's physical condition? Why had He seemed so unconcerned? Would He come to pay His respects? How should they respond? Friends, relatives, and neighbors surrounded Mary and Martha to offer comfort in their time of grief, but these two sisters couldn't get their minds off Jesus . . . or their brother Lazarus.

Then a close friend ran into the house and whispered to Mary and Martha, "I just saw Jesus and His disciples walking up the road from the Judean Wilderness toward town." Mary could not bring herself to leave the house, but Martha rushed out to see the Lord.

Perhaps Martha's decision to meet Jesus as He entered the village came from her desire to be the ever-gracious hostess. Or perhaps it sprang from a deeper spiritual understanding of who Jesus was. Or perhaps it's because she was a woman of action. In any case Martha went to greet the One who, had He come just four days earlier, could have prevented Lazarus's death. Her greeting contained a mixture of faith and sadness. "Lord . . . if you had been here, my brother would not have died" (John 11:21).

Martha and Mary must have played . . . and replayed . . . the "if only" game countless times over the past few days. "If only Jesus had been here when Lazarus became ill." "If only Jesus had arrived in time to heal our brother." "If only . . . " The words became such a frequent refrain that both sisters greeted the Lord the same way. When Mary later went out to meet Jesus, the first words from her lips were, "Lord, if you had been here, my brother would not have died" (John 11:32).

Two sisters consumed with grief. Stressed out by circumstances beyond their control. Struggling with disappointment. But Martha kept her sense of balance. Several important differences between Mary and Martha highlight Martha's ability to maintain perspective in this particular instance.

- Mary stayed home while Martha went out to meet Jesus (11:20).
- Mary focused only on what Jesus could have done in the past (11:32) while Martha added, "But I know that even now God will give you whatever you ask" (11:21–22).
- Mary was consumed with grief (11:33) while Martha gained strength from the certainty of a future resurrection and her trust in Jesus as "the Christ, the Son of God" (11:24, 27).

The specific details of Jesus' encounter with Mary and Martha are significant. In this particular event, Martha is the sister with the greater sense of balance and perspective. Both believed Jesus could have healed Lazarus while he was still alive. But once Lazarus died, Mary could only grieve. Martha, however, found stability by seeking out Jesus and trusting in His ability to solve life's problems.

Martha revealed her faith through her three confessions

to Jesus. First, she believed Jesus could alter events and circumstances . . . even death. Benjamin Franklin wrote, "Nothing is certain but death and taxes." Death is the last great unalterable. As long as there is life, there is hope. But can hope extend on into the grave? Martha's answer was, Yes! Lazarus had been dead four days, "But I know that even now God will give you whatever you ask."

Second, Martha believed her separation from Lazarus was only temporary. Her brother would live again. The pain and heartache she now felt would someday vanish, and God would reunite her with her brother. "I know he will rise again in the resurrection at the last day."

Third, Martha believed Jesus was the promised Messiah who was also God's Son. Bible teachers focus on Peter's great confession at Caesarea Philippi. "You are the Christ, the Son of the living God" (Matthew 16:16). But few notice this deep woman of faith from Bethany came to the same settled conviction. "I believe that you are the Christ, the Son of God, who was to come into the world" (John 11:27).

Martha could believe in Jesus' ability to influence the future because she understood who Jesus was. He was not just a good man. He was not just a prophet. He was not just a teacher. He was not just a miracle worker. He was Israel's Messiah, and He was the eternal Son of God.

THE CROWD WAITED IN CURIOUS ANTICIPATION AS JESUS AND THE SISTERS WENT TO THE GRAVE.

How big is your Jesus? Do you believe He can make a genuine change in life's struggles? Do you believe He will someday be able to wipe every tear from your eyes? Do you believe He is the eternal Son of God? It's so easy to forget these great truths in the middle of our struggles.

But this knowledge provides balance, enables us to endure . . . and allows us to maintain our integrity.

Martha maintained balance in her time of grief by looking beyond the physical loss of her brother to God who created life . . . who sustained life . . . and who would someday restore life. In viewing life through God's eternal perspective Martha found peace . . . yet she still had much to learn.

Now Martha wanted Mary to discover the same sense of understanding. After making her great confession, Martha "went back and called her sister Mary aside. 'The Teacher is here,' she said, 'and is asking for you'" (John 11:28). Mary went to the Lord and "fell at his feet" (John 11:32).

In each of Jesus' three visits to Bethany we find Mary kneeling at His feet. In the first visit she knelt at His feet to learn. Here she kneels at His feet to mourn. In the next visit she will kneel at His feet to worship. Mary struggled to maintain balance as she grieved over the death of her brother. But she instinctively knew she would find her answers at the feet of Jesus.

The crowd waited in curious anticipation as Jesus and the sisters went to the grave. They understood the depth of His love as they watched Him weep. They speculated what might have happened had the Master arrived before Lazarus died. And they gasped when they heard Him give the command to roll the stone away from the mouth of the tomb.

Martha spoke and expressed the thought that must have been in everyone's mind. "But, Lord . . . by this time there is a bad odor, for he has been there four days" (John 11:39). We know he's dead. Please let us remember him as he was when we put him in the tomb . . . wrapped in clean linen and covered with fragrant perfume. Don't remind us again of the awful corruption of death.

Jesus gently reminded Martha of the need to believe . . . to keep trusting in difficult times. Then He shouted, "Lazarus, come out!" Had we been there as photographers for the *Jerusalem Post*, it would have been difficult deciding which scene was more dramatic. Turn your camera to the left and photograph a man wrapped like a mummy staggering to the entrance of the tomb. Or turn your camera to the right and catch the faces of the crowd watching Lazarus come from the tomb. Eyes wide open . . . jaws hanging slack . . . bodies frozen in place . . . hands half raised in fright and amazement.

After a few startled moments, Martha and Mary must have rushed over to release their brother from the grave clothes . . . the last vestiges of death still holding Lazarus in their grip. Mourning turned to feasting as the sisters welcomed their brother back from the grave. And they understood the importance of trusting God to maintain stability and balance in a chaotic world. God's eternal power is not reserved only for the "sweet bye and bye," it's available to us in the stressful here and now.

ALMOST MISSING THE WORSHIP OF GOD

Two visits to the home of Mary and Martha. Two very different occasions. Two women growing in their faith who each demonstrate great balance at different times. But we must stop by the hometown of these remarkable women one more time. It's early spring, and the Mount of Olives is covered with a carpet of green grass, punctuated by small patches of red and yellow flowers. The sky is blue, and the temperature is already beginning to warm. People are scurrying around cleaning their homes and purging them of leaven. Passover is just six days away.

Tomorrow Jesus will ride a colt down the Mount of Olives into Jerusalem as thousands of cheering Jews cry, "Hosanna!

Blessed is he who comes in the name of the Lord!" (John 12:12–13). Five days later Jesus will be crucified. But tonight the mood is relaxed and festive. Jesus is attending a banquet given in His honor. John does not tell us where in Bethany the banquet was held, but Matthew reports it took place in "the home of a man known as Simon the Leper." Perhaps the banquet was given by Simon or his family to honor the One who had healed him of his leprosy.

The banquet may have been held in Simon's home, but Mary, Martha, and Lazarus all attended. "Martha served, while Lazarus was among those reclining at the table" (John 12:2). Somehow I expected to find Martha serving!

The banquet in Bethany must have been a grand affair. In addition to Simon the leper, Jesus, and Lazarus, the guests included Jesus' disciples and "a large crowd of Jews" who came to see Jesus and Lazarus. In a typical banquet style adopted from the Greeks and Romans the guests reclined around the outside of a low table shaped like the capital letter E with the middle bar removed. A large crowd of uninvited guests had also arrived, eager to catch a glimpse of Jesus and Lazarus. They were pushing their way from the outer courtyard into the banquet hall, making it difficult for those serving to reach the guests. Each guest reclined on mats or pillows with his feet angling away from the table. He leaned on his left elbow while eating with his right hand. Martha and the other servers would bring the food to the inside of the table to serve.

All the activity focused around the table facing toward the inside. I suspect no one even saw Mary slip around the outside of the table toward Jesus' feet. Perhaps it took a few seconds before one of the guests paused, sniffed the air, and looked around to see the source of the strong odor filling the room. There was Mary on her knees pouring nearly a pint of pure nard on the feet of Jesus!

Nard, a fragrant oil, was normally applied in small quantities to the head. The apostle John carefully notes Mary used "pure nard, an expensive perfume" (John 12:3). How expensive? Judas, the "treasurer" did a quick mental calculation. A pint of pure nard sold for about three hundred denarii, a "year's wages" for the average worker in Judea.

Judas feigned concern over Mary's extravagance. "Why wasn't this perfume sold and the money given to the poor?" (John 12:5). However, John records Judas's real motive. "He did not say this because he cared about the poor but because he was a thief; as keeper of the money bag, he used to help himself to what was put into it" (John 12:6). Judas said all the right words . . . for all the wrong reasons!

But while John focuses on Judas and his motives, another gospel writer, Matthew, takes a critical look at the other disciples. Evidently, they were swayed by Judas's reasoning. "When the disciples saw this [perfume being poured out], they were indignant. 'Why this waste?' they asked" (Matthew 26:8). They were in the "do good deeds for the kingdom" business, and Mary's actions seemed like a big waste of money. They were out of balance.

What's more important than serving God . . . doing good . . . helping others? The disciples knew the importance of serving others and, with the exception of hypocritical Judas, they felt the perfume could have been better used for God's glory by being sold. I'm sure they were indignant as they protested loudly, "How could this woman be so thoughtless in her extravagance!" They missed the point . . . but Jesus was about to set them straight.

All heads snapped back to Jesus when He spoke . . . and their eyebrows arched upward when He directed His rebuke at *them*! "'Leave her alone,' Jesus replied. 'It was intended that she should save this perfume for the day of my burial'" (John

12:7). The gospel of Mark adds a few additional details to Jesus' explanation. "She poured perfume on my body beforehand to prepare for my burial" (Mark 14:8).

Jesus had been announcing His coming death for some time. Numerous times He explained to His disciples "that he must go to Jerusalem and suffer many things at the hands of the elders, chief priests and teachers of the law, and that he must be killed and on the third day be raised to life" (Matthew 16:21). No one took Jesus' words seriously . . . except Mary.

Mary must have heard Jesus' pronouncements of His coming death . . . taken His words to heart . . . understood He was dying to purchase her salvation . . . and decided to show her love in one supreme act of worship. Perhaps the jar of pure nard was her most valued possession. Very likely it was her most costly. She would show her understanding, her acceptance, and her deep devotion by anointing her Lord before the time of His death and burial. This was not the impetuous action of an emotional admirer or a frivolous demonstration of conspicuous wealth. It was instead a sincere act of worship by a follower who knew . . . and believed . . . the words of her Lord.

Mary understood the necessity of balancing service with worship, but the disciples did not. Jesus' explanation must have disturbed those who had heard, but not understood, His repeated reminders of His coming death. "You will always have the poor among you, but you will not always have me" (John 12:8). Opportunities to do good, to help others, to meet needs would always exist. But opportunities to worship and serve Jesus while He was still in their midst were limited. The disciples focused so much on serving others they missed out on the opportunity they had to worship and serve the Lord.

When Jesus was asked to summarize the entire Mosaic law, He could do it in two commandments. "Love the Lord your God with all your heart and with all your soul and with all your mind" and "Love your neighbor as yourself" (Matthew 22:37–39). The entire Mosaic law hung on two commands . . . and those commands had to be kept in balance.

Some individuals claim to love God while responding to others with anger, petty jealousy, insensitivity, or indifference. They have all the right beliefs, meet at the appropriate times for worship, pray and read their Bibles diligently . . . but ignore and mistreat those around them. The apostle John summarized it well, "Let us not love with words or tongue but with actions and in truth" (1 John 3:18). How we act must be consistent with what we claim to believe.

Yet other Christians get so wrapped up in serving others they forget to worship God. They get so involved in the needs of the here-and-now that they lose sight of the God of eternity who expects—and deserves—their love and devotion. And eventually their spiritual lives become barren and sterile. Much like the church of Ephesus described by the apostle John in the book of Revelation, you can get so busy with "your deeds, your hard work and your perseverance" that you wake up one day and realize "you have forsaken your first love" (Revelation 2:2, 4). Activity, even noble service for the Lord, can become a mistress that draws our heart away from God. And if it does, our life will fly out of balance, and we will lose our integrity.

Mary understood. Jesus was more important than her possessions, more important than her reputation, more important than her service to others. He deserved her worship and devotion . . . and she put Him first.

LESSONS FROM BETHANY

We stand beside Mary and Martha waving good-bye as Jesus and His disciples depart from Bethany for the climb over the Mount of Olives to Jerusalem. The scent of nard still lingers in the house long after Jesus is gone. The broken pieces of the alabaster jar sit on a shelf in the corner, delicate reminders of their last banquet in Bethany with Jesus.

As the two sisters reflect on the Master's visits to their village and their home, they discuss the lessons they have learned. And the word that comes to mind most often is "balance." Jesus taught them several important secrets for living a balanced life in a very unbalanced world.

Martha smiles as she admits her "workaholic" nature often caused her to become distracted and frustrated . . . until Jesus reminded her of her need to balance activity with time for God and His Word.

Mary's eyes glisten and a single tear slides down her cheek as she remembers how upset she had been when Lazarus died. She refused to leave the house and meet the Lord . . . until Jesus personally sent for her. He taught her to trust in Him and to seek Him out when the stresses of life became too great to bear.

The sisters hug each other as they think about the events of the previous night. The disciples were so preoccupied with doing good . . . watching the bottom line . . . harboring resources . . . that they forgot their first love. Martha served, but Mary worshiped. And in doing so she revealed how much she understood that God's plan for His Messiah led toward the cross.

Just then a faint commotion could be heard in the distance. The crowd surging into Jerusalem chants something in unison. Both sisters strain to hear the words. "Hosanna! Blessed is he who comes in the name of the Lord!" Thousands of pilgrims shouting their support for Jesus, Israel's Messiah. But Mary—and Martha—know that at that moment Jesus is riding toward a cross, not the earthly kingdom of David. His only crown would be a crown of thorns piercing His forehead.

These two sisters maintained their balance in a week that took others from messianic expectations to desertion and denial. But they kept their balance because the Master had taught them well.

Reflect and Respond

Balance is our ability to keep from going to extremes. Several elements characterize an individual who maintains a balanced Christian life.

1. A balanced Christian life is a life that includes time spent with God and His Word. How much time do you spend "at the feet of Jesus" each day studying His Word? Are you, like Martha, too busy to spend time with Him? Choose "the better part" and establish a set time each day when you can study God's Word and pray.

2. A balanced Christian life is a life that views problems and disappointments from God's eternal perspective. Make a list of your personal frustrations and struggles. Is God big enough to take care of these problems? Ask Him to do so, and seek to understand His eternal perspective.

3. A balanced Christian life is a life that will not allow materialism to hinder the worship of God. To what extent have you used your personal possessions to demonstrate your love for God?

4. Memorize Ecclesiastes 3:1 and ask God to help you discover the proper "time" and "season" in your life for all activities . . . so you can lead a balanced life.

"It is good to grasp the one and not let go of the other. The man who fears God will avoid all extremes."
(Ecclesiastes 7:18)

STAND STILL . . . AND REFUSE TO
RETREAT. LOOK AT IT AS GOD LOOKS AT
IT AND DRAW UPON HIS POWER TO HOLD
UP UNDER THE BLAST.

—*Charles R. Swindoll*

8

THE RIGHT STUFF:
Sexual Purity

THE NAMES HAVE BEEN
CHANGED TO PROTECT THE INNOCENT

While growing up I loved watching the police shows on television that were based on true stories. One program would begin, "The story you are about to see is true. The names have been changed to protect the innocent." Well, the same is true of the story I'm about to share. The names . . . and some details . . . are changed to protect innocent individuals, churches, and groups. But the story is tragically true.

"John" grew up in a good, moral home. He was the typical boy next door a mother wants her daughter to date . . . clean-cut, friendly, outgoing, handsome, intelligent, churchgoing. After graduating in the top 10 percent of his high school class John went to his state's public university. There he started dating "Christy" a vibrant Christian woman who had also enrolled at the university. They first met in a meeting organized by one of several Christian groups on campus.

John and Christy seemed to be the model couple. Both were outspoken Christians who regularly attended church and who became highly involved in the campus group where they had first met. Both enjoyed backpacking and cycling. Both took their studies seriously and did well academically. No one was surprised when John and Christy announced their engagement at the end of their junior year.

John and Christy completed college and got married the same summer. They both found jobs in another city, moved their meager possessions, found a church where they felt comfortable, and started their new life as husband and wife. Both became actively involved in their new church, and the people loved them. They seemed like the perfect role models for the youth . . . a good example of how God intended marriage to work. The "icing on the cake" came a few years later when their first child was born.

But all was not well in John's life. He harbored secrets he was too ashamed even to share with Christy, secrets that dated back to his first year at the university. The campus had over 20,000 students, and was located near a large city. The size of the campus and the city gave John an opportunity to explore "the other side of life" in anonymity. It began with easy access to pornography. John found sexual release masturbating as he stared at the pictures of naked women.

John's fascination with "soft-core" pornography produced an intense, but short-lived, pleasure. Eventually all the naked bodies looked the same. His level of sexual satisfaction dropped. John then sought more "hard-core" pornography. The pictures and videos included men and women engaging in sexual acts. Again John felt the rush of intense sexual pleasure . . . and again it gradually faded with time.

Like a drug user being forced to take ever-increasing doses of narcotics to achieve the same high, John found his appetite for more sexually explicit material growing. He started slipping into gentlemen's clubs that featured "adult" entertainment. The need for more explicit images to reach the same level of physical satisfaction continued. Though he knew it was wrong, John even tried to convince Christy to engage in premarital sex to satisfy his growing appetite. She refused, and her stand for what he knew in his heart was right flooded him with guilt.

He went home from those dates and threw himself on his bed in tears vowing to the Lord he would never look at another pornographic picture or video . . . but he always did. No one knew of his secret life, so he had no one to hold him accountable. He finally rationalized his obsession with pornography by convincing himself it was only a temporary tool to satisfy his sexual urges until he and Christy got married. Then he wouldn't need to look at any more pornography.

During the first six months of their marriage John avoided all pornographic material. His physical relationship with Christy was as pleasing as he had always imagined it would be. It all seemed to be turning out okay . . . until John found himself home alone one evening watching a movie on television. Though the television station edited the movie for content, the sexual overtones brought back the arousal John had felt when he watched pornographic videos. He found himself mentally replaying those earlier films that had burned themselves into his memory.

Within a week John was back viewing pornography. He waited for the sexual arousal . . . but after masturbating he felt disappointed. Having held a real woman in his arms, the video images no longer brought the same sense of satisfaction. The beast within him was again growing and demanding to be fed . . . but now it would take more than mere pictures or videos to satisfy his addiction.

Some men have extramarital affairs to fill their unresolved sexual fantasies. Others seek out prostitutes. For some reason John took an even more vile and despicable route—rape.

"THE POLICE MUST HAVE THE WRONG MAN! IT CAN'T BE JOHN— WE KNOW JOHN!"

Perhaps his decision came because all the pictures and videos presented women as nothing more than sex objects designed to fulfill a man's basest needs. Perhaps his decision came because he sought anonymity for his actions. Perhaps his decision came because even prostitutes were reluctant to perform the sex acts he had seared on his mind. For whatever reason, John began stalking innocent women.

The police knew they had a serial rapist on their hands.

Same part of town each time, same basic method of entry, same perverted need to show pornographic videos to the victims before the rape. But no one suspected John . . . until the night he was caught.

One alert apartment dweller saw someone in the shadows and called the police. The police arrested John before he even realized they were closing in. "There must be some mistake!" he protested as they handcuffed him and took him to the station to be booked. His colleagues at work, his neighbors, and his friends at church could not believe the charges. "The police must have the wrong man! It can't be John—we know John!"

And Christy was shocked and devastated.

But the police had the right man. His fingerprints matched those taken from the apartments where the previous rapes had been committed, and his DNA found on his victims proved his guilt. Everything John had struggled so hard to hide in the dark recesses of his "other life" now made the front page of the local newspaper.

At the trial John's family had to endure painfully graphic testimony of the vile things he had done. The "other side" of John was dirty and ugly. As victim after victim took the stand to testify, the horror of his actions grew. Innocent lives marred and scarred to satisfy the basest needs of a man who worked so hard to present himself to others as a model Christian.

Today John sits in a cell in a maximum security prison. His family is shattered, his children are growing up without their father in the home, his church friends still struggle with feelings of hurt and anger. Much like a mudslide sweeping down a hill, John's arrest, trial, and conviction swept away his façade of decency and exposed the sin that lurked just beneath the surface.

Your first response to John's tragic life might be, "It could never happen to me." And in one sense you are probably correct. Most individuals do not resort to such extreme acts. But be careful before you lower your guard. You *are* vulnerable to sexual temptation. And the consequences can be just as deadly to your physical, emotional, and spiritual health.

The apostle Paul wrote to the church in Corinth, which was struggling with serious moral, personal, and interpersonal problems. In the middle of his letter he taught the people of Corinth a history lesson that focused on the children of Israel in the wilderness. Paul reminded his readers that a number of sins (including "sexual immorality") destroyed an entire generation of Israelites in the wilderness (1 Corinthians 10:6–11). He then applied this lesson to the church in Corinth. "So, if you think you are standing firm, be careful that you don't fall!" (1 Corinthians 10:12).

But why devote an entire chapter to the danger of sexual immorality and the need for sexual purity? Isn't lying . . . or pride . . . or greed just as bad? In one sense it's true that all sin is evil in God's sight. Every sin is an affront to God's holiness. And yet, we must focus on the importance of sexual purity for two reasons.

First, the Bible says there is a sense in which sexual sins are in a different class from most other sins. Paul explained this distinction to the church at Corinth . . . a city with a reputation for sexual excess. (One euphemism for a prostitute in Paul's day was a "Corinthian girl.") Paul cut through the niceties and underscored the bottom line. "Flee from sexual immorality. All other sins a man commits are outside his body, but he who sins sexually sins against his own body. Do you not know that your body is a temple of the Holy Spirit, who is in you, whom you have received from God?" (1 Corinthians 6:18–19). Sexual sins desecrate God's living temples on earth.

Second, we must focus on sexual purity because sexual temptation in our society is rampant . . . and growing exponentially. A few years ago parents worried about "girlie" magazines flaunting bare breasts or movies that presented sexually suggestive scenes. Today every conceivable type of pornography is freely available to anyone with an Internet connection. We live in a society in which condoms are distributed in school clinics and where the idea that schools should teach abstinence as an answer to teenage pregnancy and AIDS is ridiculed. Sexually transmitted diseases are increasing at an alarming rate among today's teenagers . . . and the only sure solution is sexual purity.

Christians can become desensitized to the danger by all the sexual images bombarding them every day. Much like the proverbial frog in the kettle, we don't realize the effect all the advertising and programming is having on us . . . until it's too late. The number of Christians falling into the trap of sexual immorality is too great to ignore. And the results are catastrophic!

TAKING PERSONAL RESPONSIBILITY

Society has elevated "victimhood" to unprecedented heights. We are not to blame for our actions because we are "victims" of our ethnic background, family dysfunction, economic social, or educational disadvantages. If anyone ever had the opportunity to justify his actions by claiming to be such a victim, it was Joseph. His story, recorded in Genesis 37–45, is an important reminder that life is a mixture of circumstances that are often beyond our control—and our response to those circumstances, which is within our control.

Joseph chose to respond appropriately, regardless of his circumstances.

Joseph was born into a home that we would euphemistically call "blended," but that might better be described as dysfunctional. The quarrels, plots, deception, intrigue, and infighting among this extended family sound like a modern-day soap opera. Joseph's father, Jacob, had two wives and two concubines, each of whom bore him children.

Jacob was a weak, ineffective husband and father. His daughter Dinah was raped, but he kept quiet about it and refused to act (Genesis 34:5). Instead, he got upset with two of his sons when they acted to avenge this evil deed (Genesis 34:6–7, 25–31). Jacob's oldest son had sexual relations with one of Jacob's concubines, and though Jacob knew of it, he did not rebuke his son at that time (Genesis 35:22). Joseph grew up with a father who did not model character or strength of conviction.

Joseph could also claim to be a victim of interpersonal conflict with his brothers. As the firstborn son of Jacob's favorite wife, Joseph received special attention from his father.

The breaking point for the brothers came when Jacob gave Joseph "a richly ornamented robe" signaling his favoritism toward Joseph. "When his brothers saw that their father loved him [Joseph] more than any of them, they hated him [Joseph] and could not speak a kind word to him" (Genesis 37:4).

BY TODAY'S STANDARDS JOSEPH HAD EVERY RIGHT TO BE BITTER AND ANGRY.

Jacob's unwise actions caused his other sons to ostracize Joseph. The more Jacob showered Joseph with special praise, the more resentful Joseph's brothers became. Their hatred boiled over when Jacob sent Joseph to check on them. "But they saw him in the distance, and before he reached them, they plotted to kill him" (Genesis 37:18).

To the brothers the location must have seemed ideal. In their search for suitable grazing land they had traveled seventy miles from their father's tent in the Valley of Hebron (Genesis 37:14–17). No one knew Jacob—or his sons—in this part of the land. Even if someone discovered Joseph's body, they wouldn't know who he was—or where he was from. And the main travelers along the pathway were Midianite merchants plying their trade between Egypt and Mesopotamia.

The brothers did not follow through with their initial plan. Instead, they sold Joseph as a slave to a band of traders who dragged him off to Egypt. Joseph went from being the favorite son of his father to being a foreign slave in Egypt. His journey into slavery took him "to Potiphar, one of Pharaoh's officials, the captain of the guard" (Genesis 37:36).

By today's standards Joseph had every right to be bitter and angry. His family background was complex, his father's passivity and favoritism had brought disharmony and hatred. Now he had been rejected and abandoned by his brothers . . . sold as a slave . . . stripped of his dignity . . . dragged to a foreign culture with new values and expectations. Joseph had every excuse needed to justify giving up on God and living a life of self-indulgence or self-pity. Instead, he maintained a life of purity and devotion. Let's go behind the scenes to see how he did it.

Joseph Accepted God's Standards

From favored son to slave! In a matter of weeks Joseph went from his father's large, goat hair tent with its woven carpets and numerous servants . . . to the bottom of a dank, dark cistern . . . to slavery in the house of a governmental official in Egypt. But Joseph never lost his faith in God . . . and God never abandoned Joseph. The book of Genesis states clearly, "The Lord was with Joseph and he prospered" (Genesis 39:2).

Joseph's exemplary attitude, and the success he seemed to have in every task he was given, didn't escape Potiphar's notice. "Potiphar put him in charge of his household, and he entrusted to his care everything he owned" (Genesis 39:4). In today's terms, Joseph was a winner! He went from the lowest entry-level position to upper management.

But Joseph's success was not based on the power of positive thinking. It came directly from the hand of God. Joseph put God first in his life, and God took care of the rest. Count how many times God gets the credit for Joseph's success.

- "The Lord was with Joseph" (39:2).
- "The Lord was with him" (39:3).
- "The Lord gave him success in everything he did" (39:3).
- "The Lord blessed the household of the Egyptian because of Joseph" (39:5).
- "The blessing of the Lord was on everything" (39:5).

God blessed Joseph for his faithfulness, and Joseph's life took on a "rags-to-riches" quality that must have astounded those who knew him when he first arrived in Egypt as a seventeen-year-old slave. Joseph now ran the estate of one of Egypt's most powerful officials. He also developed physically. The awkward youth who came to Egypt was now "well-built and handsome" (Genesis 39:6).

Good-looking ... successful ... self-assured ... winsome. Joseph's qualities won him many admirers, including one who had no business looking! Potiphar's wife soon "took notice of Joseph" (Genesis 39:7). Subtlety was not her strong suit. "Come to bed with me!" she ordered (39:7). She made Joseph an offer she felt he couldn't refuse.

Stop and put yourself in Joseph's place. Your family background contains polygamy, incest, and rape. Not the sort of history that instills strong moral character and convictions. The God your father claimed to serve had allowed you to be sold as a slave. Why should you listen to Him? You've been working hard, and your effort is finally starting to pay off. And now a powerful woman is throwing herself at you sexually. She wants you! Says she *needs* you! Satisfy her and she could open up countless avenues for advancement. Why not? Anyone else would.

I suspect all these thoughts flashed through Joseph's mind in the few seconds following this woman's brazen offer. Joseph blinked . . . looked away . . . and then refused her offer. Turned her down. Stopped her advance cold! Joseph stayed sexually pure by rejecting an offer that had to be hard to resist. How did he do it?

The Bible offers two reasons Joseph refused to have sexual relations with Potiphar's wife. The first reason involved trust. Potiphar had entrusted Joseph with great responsibility. "Everything he owns he has entrusted to my care. . . . My master has withheld nothing from me except you, because you are his wife" (Genesis 39:8–9). Having sexual relations with this woman would violate a trust Potiphar had placed in Joseph. Joseph could not bring himself to break that trust.

But Joseph had a second reason for refusing this woman's offer, a reason even more compelling. "How then could I do such a wicked thing and sin against God?" (Genesis 39:9). God established His standards for sexual purity and marital faithfulness at creation. To commit adultery with another man's wife was a "wicked thing" and a violation of God's moral standards. As such it was a "sin against God." Joseph looked at her offer through God's eyes and saw its perversity.

By accepting God's standards for moral conduct, Joseph saw the offer as the sin it really was.

How would you have responded had you been in that house in Joseph's place? Let's update the scene to make it more realistic for today. You are flying to another town for a job interview. On the airplane you talk to the person sitting next to you . . . and find this person to be charming and witty—to say nothing of being incredibly good looking! You smile and say good-bye as you walk up the jet ramp into the terminal.

Imagine your surprise later in the day when you meet this individual again . . . in the lobby of the office building where you have your interview. And then you learn this person is chief operating officer of the organization. Your meeting is highly successful, and when it's over the individual invites you to dinner. The meal is delightful, the conversation relaxed and friendly. You are having such a wonderful time you are mildly surprised when you discover your host is not only warm and friendly, this person seated across from you is also married, incredibly wealthy . . . and very lonely.

As the candles flicker softly, your host reaches across the table and caresses your hand. Speaking almost in a whisper the individual says, "I'm almost embarrassed to say this to you, but you are incredibly sexy and attractive. I find myself being drawn to you physically. I know this will sound forward, but I would very much like to spend the night with you."

You have nothing to lose. You enjoy this person's company. You know this night could open up great opportunities for personal advancement. None of your friends will ever know. As the sea of sexual fantasy churns around you, where can you drop your moral anchor to give you stability? Joseph teaches us that our moral anchor must rest on the bedrock of God's absolute standards of right and wrong. Sexual immorality is wrong, and those who commit immorality sin against God.

Question: How do you swallow an elephant?

Answer: One bite at a time.

Sometimes silly statements contain a great deal of truth. On the positive side, you can often accomplish a project that seems too difficult by breaking it down into smaller pieces. As I started writing this book the breadth of the subject discouraged me. But when I decided to tackle the project "one chapter at a time" it eventually came together.

But this truth has a darker side. Christians who might never agree to plunge completely into a life of sin are often enticed into that sin "one bite at a time." Few individuals go directly from a life of sexual purity to gross sexual immorality. Small choices litter the pathway to sexual immorality . . . little compromises . . . incremental movements that take the individual ever closer toward the edge. The major temptations are easy to spot, the incremental compromises are often more subtle.

> WERE THE DANGER OF SEXUAL SIN NOT SO SERIOUS, WE COULD ALMOST FIND JOSEPH'S ACTIONS COMICAL.

Joseph said no to Potiphar's wife, but she refused to take no for an answer. Her motto must have been, "If at first you don't succeed, try, try again!" She made the same offer to Joseph "day after day" (Genesis 39:10). I assume she tried slight variations on the same basic theme. One day she wore her most revealing dress . . . the next day she spent extra time putting on her makeup . . . the next day she used the most fragrant perfumes . . . the next day she tried a subtle touch as she whispered in his ear. The approach varied, but the offer never changed.

"Come to bed with me!" Potiphar's wife intended to get Joseph ... even if she had to draw him in "one bite at a time."

Joseph had a problem! Sexual temptation was ever present ... ever compelling ... ever available. But Joseph "refused to go to bed with her or even be with her" (Genesis 39:10); his strategy to fight off this woman's advances was to refuse them, but also to avoid her.

Were the danger of sexual sin not so serious, we could almost find Joseph's actions comical. Joseph rearranged his entire schedule to avoid being in a room alone with Potiphar's wife. If she was supervising the kitchen staff, Joseph was checking on the livestock. If she went out into the garden, he managed to find a reason to go inside to inventory the storehouse. Joseph was a wise man!

In a society saturated with sexual images and offers, it's easy for us to get sucked into sin "one bite at a time." Some who struggle with pornography still go back to websites offering free pornographic pictures or videos. Others stop to look at the magazine racks in stores. They scan the shelves ... their eyes looking for magazines that bring cheap thrills but no lasting satisfaction. Still others watch the daytime soap operas or movie channels, confusing true romance with the tawdry affairs and shallow physical relationships that spew from these programs.

So what's the danger in looking at sexually explicit photographs, seeing one graphic sex scene in a popular film, or reading such a scene in a novel? It's not as if we are having an affair ourselves, is it? Yes, it is! Sexual immorality begins in the mind, in agreeing to tolerate ... then enjoy ... then long for ... then seek out experiences God reserves for marriage.

Jesus understood the fact that sexual purity (and sexual immorality) begins in the mind and heart when He said, "You have heard that it was said, 'Do not commit adultery.' But I tell you that anyone who looks at a woman lustfully has already committed adultery with her in his heart" (Matthew 5:27–28). The attitude precedes the act. Sometimes the best defense against sexual temptation is physically to avoid those situations where we can be tempted.

To keep his mind pure Joseph avoided those situations where he could be tempted. Avoidance is a good technique for sexual purity. Only you and God know the specific areas where you struggle sexually. Admit your weakness and vow to avoid ever putting yourself in a place where you can be tempted in that area. It might change where you shop, what you watch on TV, where you place your computer, or where you go on vacation, but it's a small price to pay for sexual purity.

Joseph Refused to Give In to Sin

Joseph's plan to avoid tempting situations was fundamentally sound. Under normal circumstances, taking such precautions would do much to keep an individual pure. But Potiphar's wife was anything but normal. Joseph made an elusive target, but Potiphar's wife remained persistent . . . and cunning.

This wily woman carefully constructed her trap for Joseph. She first removed the other household servants. I imagine she sent some to the market . . . others into the fields . . . still others on insignificant, but time-consuming, errands. Joseph would be unable to run to a servant and use that individual to escape. No, this time it would just be she and Joseph in the house alone . . . and she would have him to herself.

"One day [Joseph] went into the house to attend to his duties, and none of the household servants was inside" (Genesis 39:11). The sound from Joseph's sandaled feet bounced off the empty halls and echoed back into his ears. The house was quiet . . . too quiet. At first, Joseph had focused so intently on his duties he hadn't noticed the silence. Now the eerie quiet made him stop . . . and listen. Not a sound.

Joseph put aside his work and softly began to walk through the house. Where were the servants? Why was the work not being done? Who had changed the schedule? Joseph was so preoccupied he didn't notice the shadow darting across the open doorway in front of him.

Joseph jumped as delicate but powerful hands grabbed the shoulders of his linen cloak and pulled. As the garment ripped from his body, exposing his nakedness, a sensuous, demanding voice spoke from the shadows. "Come to bed with me!" (Genesis 39:12).

Turning, Joseph saw Potiphar's wife. Her seductive dress and leering eyes left no doubt as to her intentions. She wanted sex with Joseph. Now—on her terms and in her bed! Joseph was trapped. Stripped of his clothes. Alone in the house. Facing a woman mad with passion.

Some might say, "Why bother to fight it?"

Joseph's solution was swift, dramatic . . . and effective! "But he left his cloak in her hand and ran out of the house" (Genesis 39:12). Run! Flee! Vamoose! Head for the hills! Joseph got his feet in gear and set an Egyptian record for the hundred-meter dash. And in doing so he became the world's first "streaker"—running away without even stopping to wrestle his clothes from the hand of the woman who had ripped them off his body.

When unexpected sexual temptations catch you off guard, don't take time to analyze, theorize, rationalize . . . or compromise. Get out! Immediately! The apostle Paul may have had Joseph in mind when he wrote about sexual temptations. The way to maintain sexual purity is to *flee* . . . just as Joseph did. Paul didn't mince words. His advice to those believers living in the moral cesspool called Corinth was, "Flee from sexual immorality" (1 Corinthians 6:18). Just over a decade later he gave the same advice to his young disciple, Timothy. "Flee the evil desires of youth" (2 Timothy 2:22).

What's the secret to sexual purity? Start by making God's standards your own. "Do you not know that the wicked will not inherit the kingdom of God? Do not be deceived: Neither the sexually immoral . . . nor adulterers nor male prostitutes nor homosexual offenders . . . will inherit the kingdom of God" (1 Corinthians 6:9–10). God condemns *all* forms of sexual immorality. Agree with God that sexual purity is the only acceptable standard . . . and make it your standard.

If you have made a commitment to remain sexually pure, what can you do to keep your vow? First, follow Joseph's example and avoid tempting situations. Watch your choice of television programs, movies, magazines, and websites. Don't allow yourself to get into a situation where you will be tempted. Second, if you ever find yourself in a situation where you are being tempted, flee! Get up, walk out, and put as much distance between you and the temptation as possible. Don't allow the temptation to gain a foothold in your mind.

WHAT IF I'VE ALREADY FAILED?

I'm enough of a realist to know my words have reached some of you too late to keep you from sexual impurity. Some of you struggle with an addiction to pornography. Others carry a burden of guilt from past sexual immorality, including premarital sex or adulterous affairs after marriage. What can you do if you have already crossed God's barrier and entered the forbidden zone of sexual immorality?

First, realize that God can, and does, forgive all sin . . . including the sin of sexual immorality. Our responsibility is to confess our sin . . . to acknowledge to God we were wrong and

He is right. "If we confess our sins, he is faithful and just and will forgive us our sins and purify us from all unrighteousness" (1 John 1:9). Why not stop reading right now and confess your sins to your heavenly Father? If you confess, He will forgive.

Second, commit in your heart to remain sexually pure for the rest of your life. You cannot undo your past . . . but you can choose your direction for the future. Follow the example of Joseph by committing to remain pure, avoiding tempting situations, and fleeing direct temptations.

Third, bathe your mind with God's Word. One sad reality of sexual immorality is that the sexual images are burned into our minds. Pornographic magazines, explicit movies, and extramarital sexual encounters leave lasting memories . . . and these memories can be as powerful a temptation to you as Potiphar's wife was to Joseph.

God provides a solution to the "mind pollution" you may have already suffered . . . the cleansing power of His Word. "Do not conform any longer to the pattern of this world, but be transformed by the renewing of your mind" (Romans 12:2).

Filling your mind with God's Word, hiding it in your heart, is God's method for cleansing your mind of the toxic waste left by past immorality. Psalm 119 focuses on the benefits of God's Word, especially for gaining mastery over temptation and sin. "How can a young man keep his way pure? By living according to your word" (119: 9). "Your word is a lamp to my feet and a light for my path" (119:105). "Direct my footsteps according to your word; let no sin rule over me" (119:133). Haunted by memories of past immorality? Start cleansing your mind by filling it with the Word of God.

Fourth, remember that sin has consequences. God can forgive your past sin . . . but forgiveness doesn't always eliminate sin's consequences. If you have sexual relations with someone to whom you are not married, it is sin. God can forgive the sin. However, if you contract AIDS or a sexually transmitted disease, God will not automatically take them away when you confess. You can receive God's forgiveness for committing rape, but God also ordained human government . . . and it will imprison you for your crime.

Sexual sin is serious, and the consequences can linger long after you confess and receive forgiveness. If you have sinned and have confessed to God, realize that one consequence of your sin may be a limit on your future service for Him. Be content to serve God in whatever capacity He graciously allows. Also, realize you will need to earn the trust of those you hurt most by your past failure. Make yourself accountable and prove yourself trustworthy. Earning back trust is a slow process . . . but the results are worth the effort.

Reflect and Respond

Sexual purity stands as one of the great defining characteristics of a faithful child of God. Yet many Christians struggle to remain sexually pure.

1. An axiom for today's computer age is, "Garbage in, garbage out." What you feed into your mind eventually shows up in how you live. Do you struggle with pornography? What types of magazines and movies are you reading and watching? Would you be embarrassed to have Jesus sit beside you while you read, watch TV, or visit a website? Avoid all the magazines, television programs, and Internet sites that can't pass the Jesus test.

2. Are you now experiencing any sexual temptations? What specifically can you do to avoid these situations? Seek out an individual you can trust and ask him or her to hold you accountable in this area.

3. Are you guilty of past sexual immorality? If so, have you confessed your sin to God? Make a specific commitment, right now, to live the rest of your life in sexual purity.

4. Memorize 1 Corinthians 6:18 and ask God to give you the ability to flee all sexual immorality from now on.

"The body is not meant for sexual immorality, but for the Lord, and the Lord for the body." (1 Corinthians 6:13b)

IF GOD SENDS US STRONG PATHS,
WE ARE PROVIDED STRONG SHOES.

—*Corrie ten Boom*

9

LACKING NOTHING:
Endurance

RUDY

Daniel "Rudy" Ruettiger transferred into Notre Dame University and tried out as a walk-on player for the Notre Dame football team. Since childhood, Rudy had dreamed of playing football for Notre Dame. Now he wanted to prove to everyone that he was a doer, not just a dreamer.

Neither the coaches nor the players believed Rudy could succeed. At 5'6" and 165 pounds he was just too small, too slow . . . too average to have any chance to make the team. But Rudy proved them all wrong. His grit, determination, and heart more than made up for his size and limited athletic ability. Rudy made the scout team . . . the group of unknowns with the thankless job of helping the main squad prepare for each week's game. Glorified tackling dummies!

Rudy threw himself into the role. Though he only had a fraction of the athletic ability of the starting players, he exerted twice the effort. His persistence and desire inspired other members of the team. For two years he served on the scout team. Bruised, beaten up, battered . . . but never broken in spirit. Rudy lived out his dream.

In the final game of his senior year the starting players persuaded the coach to allow Rudy to "suit up" for the game. In the closing seconds the coach sent him in from the sidelines, and Rudy made one spectacular play. As the game ended the other players hoisted Rudy on their shoulders and carried him off the field. Rudy was a winner!

Rudy Ruettiger's inspiring story touches a tender spot in all our hearts. We *like* stories that focus on individuals who endure in spite of adversity . . . who persevere to overcome great obstacles. The true story of Rudy made a wonderful motion picture. And as a speaker and corporate trainer he is *still* motivating people to strive to be their best.

WHAT'S WRONG WITH THIS PICTURE?

We love stories of individuals who overcome and persevere . . . but our perception is often distorted. We focus on the "happy ending" and forget the pain and struggle it took to get there. We imagine ourselves being hoisted onto the shoulders of the other Notre Dame players and forget the two years of physical punishment and pounding Rudy Ruettiger endured to earn the right to sit on those shoulders.

A little bit of Walter Mitty lives in us all. Walter Mitty is James Thurber's fictional character who spent most of his dreary life daydreaming about great exploits . . . starring himself as the hero, of course! Walter Mitty dreamed great dreams, but he never bridged the chasm between dreaming and doing. The world has a surplus of Walter Mitty's . . . and a shortage of Rudy Ruettigers.

What separates the dreamers from the doers? One big difference is endurance. All of us dream, but few are willing to pay the price required to make those dreams reality. When the going gets tough, most stop going! Endurance is the ability to stay the course . . . to pay the price . . . to keep going when everyone else says it's time to quit.

> SOMETIMES IT HELPS OUR OWN UNDERSTANDING OF THE BIBLE IF WE TRANSLATE GOD'S THOUGHTS INTO THE LANGUAGE OF TODAY.

WHEN THE GOING GETS TOUGH

The prophet Jeremiah served God at a time when God's prophets were not popular. The people of Judah refused to respond to Jeremiah's call to repent. One time Jeremiah thought the people were about to respond. But God opened his eyes to the harsh reality of human sinfulness. "I had been like a gentle lamb led to the slaughter; I did not realize that they had plotted against me" (Jeremiah 11:19).

Sweet Jeremiah suddenly saw behind the smiling faces and understood what the people actually thought of him, his message, and his God. Jeremiah cried out in discouragement, and God reminded him of the need for endurance. "If you have raced with men on foot and they have worn you out, how can you compete with horses? If you stumble in safe country, how will you manage in the thickets by the Jordan?" (Jeremiah 12:5).

Sometimes it helps our own understanding of the Bible if we translate God's thoughts into the language of today. God threw a cold bucket of reality on Jeremiah and said, "Jeremiah, if you are struggling to make it through the Boston Marathon, what will you do when I enter you in the Kentucky Derby? If you stumble on rock-covered roads, what will you do when I hand you a machete and have you hack your way through impenetrable jungle? Prepare yourself, Jeremiah. It will get harder before it gets easier!"

So how would you feel if you were Jeremiah? (Anyone who says "Great!" needs to go back and read the chapter on honesty!) None of us likes pain, struggle, or hardship. But sometimes that is the only way God can accomplish His work in us . . . and use us to make an impact on others.

IT IS WELL

Hanging in the lobby of Jerusalem's American Colony Hotel is a handwritten poem. Neither the penmanship nor the paper give this poem its special place on the wall. Its author,

Horatio Spafford, scratched out the words on a blank sheet of hotel stationery. The poem is special because of the grandeur of its thoughts . . . and the circumstances that led to its writing.

Philip Bliss later set the words to music, and the song "It Is Well with My Soul" remains a classic Christian song of hope. Of all the Christian songs I know, this simple song by Spafford and Bliss touches my soul like no other. What prompted Spafford to write the words of the song . . . and how those words ended up on the lobby wall of this venerable Jerusalem hotel is an intriguing story.

Horatio Spafford lived in Chicago in the late 1800s. Friends would describe Spafford as a family man, a lawyer . . . and a Christian. Yet within the space of two short years this Christian gentleman saw his world collapse. In October 1871, the Great Chicago Fire wiped out Chicago's central business district . . . including Spafford's law offices. The fire also devastated Chicago's economy, threatening several real estate ventures in which Spafford had invested heavily. One year later these ventures failed. Both the fire and the real estate failure hurt Horatio Spafford financially. But the worst was yet to come.

Spafford sent his wife and four children on a trip to Europe while he tried to put his personal finances back in order. His family set sail on the *Ville du Harve*, one of the premier passenger ships sailing the Atlantic Ocean. But on November 21, 1873, the *Ville du Harve* was struck by another vessel and sank in the cold waters of the North Atlantic. Spafford's wife miraculously survived the shipwreck . . . but all four children were lost at sea. The cable Spafford received from his wife described the magnitude of their loss in a few simple words: SAVED ALONE. WHAT SHALL I DO.

As soon as he received the cable, Spafford boarded a train for the East Coast to book passage on the next available ship.

He wanted . . . he needed . . . to be with his wife in this time of sorrow and tragedy. During the journey across the Atlantic the captain summoned Spafford to his cabin as the ship reached the spot where the *Ville du Harve* had gone down.

Stop and put yourself in Horatio Spafford's place. Grief stricken. Alone. Financially drained. Physically drained. Emotionally drained. How would you fare under the hammer blows of trouble he had faced? When all life's crutches and supports are kicked away, how well would you be able to stand?

Horatio Spafford left us two written records that serve as windows into his soul during this dark, lonely period. The first is a letter he wrote to a sister-in-law.

> On Thursday last we passed over the spot where she went down, in mid-ocean, the water three miles deep. But I do not think of our dear ones there. They are safe, folded, the dear lambs, and there, before very long, shall we be too. In the meantime, thanks to God, we have an opportunity to serve and praise Him for His love and mercy to us and ours. "I will praise Him while I have my being." May we each one arise, leave all, and follow Him.[13]

Pause for just a second and read those words again . . . slowly. How could Horatio Spafford speak of "love," "mercy," and "praise" in such a time of sorrow? What gave him the ability to thank God in the midst of personal pain? How could he endure such heartache . . . and then turn tragedy into triumph?

Spafford shared his secret in his other writing . . . his poem that now hangs in the hotel lobby. In this poem Spafford opened his heart as he put his thoughts to verse. Imagine for a moment you are Horatio Spafford, and read these words as if you had just written them on a piece of hotel stationery with your fountain pen.

When peace like a river attendeth my way,
When sorrows like sea-billows roll;
Whatever my lot, Thou has taught me to say,
"It is well, it is well with my soul."

Though Satan should buffet, though trials should come,
Let this blest assurance control,
That Christ hath regarded my helpless estate,
And hath shed His own blood for my soul.

My sin—O, the bliss of this glorious thought,
My sin, not in part but the whole,
Is nailed to His cross and I bear it no more,
Praise the Lord, praise the Lord, O my soul!

And, Lord, haste the day when the faith shall be sight,
The clouds be rolled back as a scroll,
The trump shall resound, and the Lord shall descend,
A song in the night, oh my soul![14]

How could Spafford respond with such assurance, joy, and peace? His was not a natural response. God had *taught* him to say, "It is well with my soul." He endured because he grasped God's purpose, God's protection, and God's plan in the events that seemed to swirl out of control all around him.

WELL DONE, THOU GOOD AND FAITHFUL SERVANT

Several years ago I heard Spafford's haunting words, and my eyes misted over as a lump formed in the back of my throat. I had just delivered a eulogy for Bob Sturges, a dear friend who had died in an automobile accident, and the soloist who followed me sang "It Is Well with My Soul." I sat on the platform looking out into the audience, but my eyes kept drifting back to the closed coffin just below me. I stared at the wooden box that held the earthly remains of a remarkable man. It seemed as if much of Odessa, Texas, agreed with me because the church was full of friends who had come to say good-bye.

What was it about this man that allowed him to make such an impact on others? From my own experience I felt confident it was Bob's character and integrity. He was quiet . . . unassuming . . . humble . . . compassionate . . . caring . . . thorough . . . committed to excellence. When I read through some of the cards and letters before the service, I saw phrases like "an inspiration to teachers," "a model for others," "an influence to me," and "an encourager."

This dear saint, and his wonderful wife, made an impact on others because they consistently lived for Jesus Christ. In good times . . . and bad. In easy times . . . and hard. In times of joy . . . and sorrow. In times of ease . . . and struggle. They endured . . . and triumphed! Two days before the accident that ultimately took his life, Bob shared with a friend his confidence that we live each day preparing ourselves for eternity . . . and he was prepared. Much like Enoch in the Old Testament, he "walked with God; then he was no more, because God took him away" (Genesis 5:24).

Bob's life could be summarized in three words. He endured . . . persevered . . . and triumphed. From a human perspective his life ended suddenly—abruptly. But God doesn't make mistakes. This man of God lived every moment of his life as if it might be his last, and he was ready when God called him to heaven. As I sat on the platform of the church, I wiped a tear from my cheek and thought about the first words he may have heard when he opened his eyes in heaven. Perhaps words like,

"Well done, thou good and faithful servant: . . . enter thou into the joy of thy lord" (Matthew 25:21 KJV).

THE TESTING OF YOUR FAITH

James, the half brother of our Lord Jesus Christ, opened his book with startling words. Writing to those facing pain and suffering, James said, "Consider it pure joy, my brothers, whenever you face trials of many kinds, because you know that the testing of your faith develops perseverance. Perseverance must finish its work so that you may be mature and complete, not lacking anything" (James 1:2–4).

The testing of faith produces perseverance, and perseverance produces maturity. James reminded his readers that the proper response to problems will develop spiritual maturity. Perseverance is a process that produces depth of character. But words alone can ring hollow. When individuals face life-and-death situations, they often need concrete images to help them stay focused.

James understood his audience's need to see God's truth demonstrated in the lives of His followers. Later in his book James pointed his readers to flesh-and-blood examples of patience and perseverance. "Brothers, as an example of patience in the face of suffering, take the prophets who spoke in the name of the Lord. As you know, we consider blessed those who have persevered. You have heard of Job's perseverance and have seen what the Lord finally brought about" (James 5:10–11).

Many of us grew up hearing about the "patience of Job," and reading about his "patience" in the King James Version of my Bible. Then I studied Greek and learned that James actually spoke of the "perseverance of Job." James used two different words to describe "patience" and "perseverance." The "prophets who spoke in the name of the Lord" displayed "patience," and Job demonstrated "perseverance." Let's face it, Job didn't always exhibit great patience! But he does stand as a model of perseverance. Let's wander down to the ash heap to spend some time with Job and his friends.

THE PERSEVERANCE OF JOB

Job lived most of his life in power and luxury. He served as the model for *Time* magazine's "Person of the Year" before *Time* magazine ever existed. In a day when society measured wealth in livestock, Job dominated the "stock" market. He owned 7,000 sheep (he covered the clothing market), 3,000 camels (he corralled the transportation industry), and 500 yoke of oxen and 500 donkeys (he cornered the farming sector). Simply put, "He was the greatest man among all the people of the East" (Job 1:3).

But while many claw their way to the top by cutting corners or climbing over the backs of others, Job managed to reach the pinnacle of success with his integrity intact. "This man was blameless and upright; he feared God and shunned evil" (Job 1:1). Honest businessman. Faithful husband. Good father. Job was almost too good to be true, as Satan tried to convince God.

Then one tragic day, the wheels came off. We learn in the first two chapters of the book that Job was a test case in the cosmic struggle between God and Satan. Satan challenged Job's motives . . . and God's own worthiness to receive worship. "Job is only in it for the blessings You bestow," Satan charged. "Take away the blessings and see how much he really cares for You." Satan received God's permission to test Job . . . and Job never knew what hit him!

In the space of a few hours Job went from prince to pauper.

Before one messenger could finish telling Job about a disaster, another messenger arrived with still more bad news. Foreign invaders stole all the oxen and donkeys. A freak thunderstorm killed all the sheep. Foreign invaders stole all the camels. A freak storm blew over a house and killed all his children. Bam! Four hammer blows of sorrow landed directly on Job.

But Satan was not through with Job. Having stripped him of his wealth, Satan set out to rob him of his health. Satan "afflicted Job with painful sores from the soles of his feet to the top of his head" (Job 2:7). In misery and sorrow, Job "sat among the ashes." Then Satan used Job's own wife to whisper the final words of temptation when Job was most vulnerable. "Are you still holding on to your integrity? Curse God and die!" (Job 2:9).

Though spoken out of hurt, anger, and sorrow for her stricken husband and lost children, the words of Job's wife still asked a haunting question. How could Job possibly maintain his integrity after being abandoned by God? After all, in two of the first four calamities God had not stepped in to protect Job from the attacks of others. And we call the other two calamities "acts of God" . . . pointing to God Himself as the author of the evil now holding Job in its vise-like grip.

How did Job survive spiritually when the wheels came off? What gave him his stability and his ability to endure in such trying circumstances? Job provided four answers in his extended debate with those who tried to comfort him.

Endurance Comes from Looking Inward

Job remained on course spiritually because he set his internal compass properly. When he lost everything, he reminded himself that the Sovereign God who had granted him wealth also had the right to take it away. "Naked I came from my mother's womb, and naked I will depart. The Lord gave and the Lord has taken away; may the name of the Lord be praised" (Job 1:21).

Job had no idea why he was suffering. He knew nothing of the contest between God and Satan. From Job's perspective it seemed to be a case of mistaken identity. God had chosen to punish him though he was innocent. Job longed for an opportunity to meet face-to-face with God so he could clear his name. But, from Job's perspective, even if God wrongly punished him, he refused to stop living in a way that pleased God. "As surely as God lives, who has denied me justice, the Almighty, who has made me taste bitterness of soul, as long as I have life within me, the breath of God in my nostrils, my lips will not speak wickedness, and my tongue will utter no deceit" (Job 27:2–4).

Others can take your reputation, your riches, your health, and even your happiness. But no one can take away your integrity . . . except you. Job's world fell apart. Right seemed to become wrong. Up became down. Righteousness brought pain instead of blessing. When life strips away all the external rewards and controls, how would you respond? When you no longer must act a part or play a role expected by others, what would the "real" you say and do?

When Job reached the irreducible minimum, all he had left inside were his convictions and his integrity. Right *was* right, wrong *was* wrong. And Job refused to compromise on his convictions, or his integrity. his final speech to his friends ended with Job taking a series of oaths proclaiming his commitment to integrity. He began by attesting, "I made a covenant with my eyes not to look lustfully at a girl" (Job 31:1). In the following verses Job affirmed his commitment to sexual purity, honesty, justice, compassion, and faithfulness. In each case he stated on oath to God, "If I have secretly sinned in this area, may I be judged for my actions!"

Have you made a commitment similar to the one made by Job? Have you committed in your heart that, come what may, you will not depart from living a life of integrity? Whatever the temptation. Whatever the circumstances. Whatever the cost to you personally or professionally. Looking inside and setting our internal moral compass is the first step in developing endurance.

Endurance Comes from Looking Upward

Job had his internal compass set. When trouble came, he could endure because he looked inward at that compass of integrity. But he also needed a fixed point of reference to help him stay on course. Job's fixed point of reference was the character and nature of God. Job could endure because he looked to God, even if it appeared as though God had abandoned him.

When Job spoke with his three friends, their attempts to comfort provided no help at all. Job needed to speak to God. As the incessant speeches of the three friends wore on, he turned from them to seek out God. In frustration he cried out, "What you [three friends] know, I also know; I am not inferior to you. But I desire to speak to the Almighty and to argue my case with God. You, however, smear me with lies; you are worthless physicians, all of you! If only you would be altogether silent! For you, that would be wisdom" (Job 13:2–5).

Job wanted . . . needed . . . to speak with God. But from Job's perspective, God was the Author of his misfortunes. Why, then, seek out God? Ultimately it was a matter of trust. He didn't understand why God permitted him to suffer, but Job still trusted in God. "Though he slay me, yet will I hope in him; I will surely defend my ways to his face. Indeed, this will turn out for my deliverance, for no godless man would dare come before him!" (Job 13:15–16).

I find Job's faith in God remarkable. He did not know of the cosmic struggle causing his pain. (We do!) He did not possess any of God's Word to give him comfort, perspective, or hope. (We do!) He did not know God had already decreed he would not die. (We do!) He did not know God would reward his faithfulness and restore his life. (We do!) Job knew far less about God than we do, but he trusted God completely.

At one point Job cried out, "Even now my witness is in heaven; my advocate is on high. My intercessor is my friend as my eyes pour out tears to God; on behalf of a man he pleads with God as a man pleads for his friend" (Job 16:19–21). Job believed someone in heaven heard his words and presented his case to God. And that individual, whoever he was, had Job's interests at heart.

What Job only knew intuitively, we know for certain. We have *two* advocates in heaven pleading for us: God the Holy Spirit and God the Son. In Romans 8 the apostle Paul reminded his readers that "the Spirit intercedes for the saints in accordance with God's will" (Romans 8:27). The writer of Hebrews described Jesus as the "great high priest who has gone through the heavens" and who is able to "sympathize with our weaknesses" (Hebrews 4:14–15). Because of Jesus' ministry for us the writer urged his readers to go confidently before God in prayer. "Let us then approach the throne of grace with confidence, so that we may receive mercy and find grace to help us in our time of need" (Hebrews 4:16).

Job endured because he knew God was still seated on His throne, in control of all people, events, and circumstances. Job knew he could continue to trust God, and he knew God would hear, and eventually act on, his heartfelt cries. Job had no idea when . . . or how . . . God would respond. But he endured because he knew God *would* respond . . . sometime. He just had to hang on till then.

Endurance Comes from Looking Outward

Reading through the book of Job reminded me of the one and only time I drove a car in England. I vividly remember the first "roundabout," the circular intersection where roads and highways merge. I was seated on the "wrong" side of the car, driving on the "wrong" side of the highway, merging the "wrong" way on this circular roundabout . . . all the while watching for other cars and the proper exit! I concentrated so much on not hitting other drivers and on staying in the proper lane that I missed the turnoff . . . twice!

Job's three friends drove their dilapidated theological truck onto Job's roundabout, and kept going round and round. Same flawed arguments. Same incorrect conclusions. Same self-righteous sense of superiority. Job finally blurts out, "I have heard many things like these; miserable comforters are you all! Will your long-winded speeches never end? What ails you that you keep on arguing?" (Job 16:2–3).

All right! Give it to them, Job! They deserve it! The last thing we need in our time of struggle is self-appointed sages with simplistic solutions for our difficult problems. In our time of pain and hurt we are tempted to lash out at those around us . . . and these three made tempting targets. In seeking to defend God's justice they assumed Job had sinned—that somehow he deserved the punishment he appeared to be receiving.

In the end God justified Job and condemned the three friends. "I am angry with you [Eliphaz, the 'senior partner of these three stooges'] and your two friends, because you have not spoken of me what is right, as my servant Job has" (Job 42:7).

God ordered the three friends to take "seven bulls and seven rams and . . . sacrifice a burnt offering for yourselves" (Job 42:8a). Then God asked Job to *pray* for his friends. "My servant Job will pray for you, and I will accept his prayer" (Job 42:8b). I suspect Job's head shot up and furrows lined his brow as he replayed in his mind what God had just said. What! You want *me* to serve as the intercessor for my friends? These are the ones who have been harassing me!

Christ's disciples must have been as surprised as Job when they heard Jesus tell them, "You have heard that it was said, 'Love your neighbor and hate your enemy.' But I tell you: Love your enemies and pray for those who persecute you" (Matthew 5:43–44). God commands us to endure the problems and pains of this life, but He does not want our reaction to those problems and pains to hold us hostage. Harboring grudges, nursing bitterness, and holding on to hatred will imprison an individual. Locked in a cell of anger, they will allow the past to control their future.

THE KEY TO THE PASSAGE IS THE TIMING OF GOD'S RESTORATION OF JOB.

Sometimes when reading the Bible, we suddenly gain new insight on a passage we have read countless times before. The truth was always there. We just didn't notice it before. I made one such discovery in the last chapter of Job. God asked Job to pray for his friends, and Job did. "After Job had prayed for his friends, the Lord made him prosperous again and gave him twice as much as he had before" (Job 42:10). The King James Version of the Bible says the same thing, though slightly more poetically: "And the Lord turned the captivity of Job, when he prayed for his friends."

The key to the passage is the timing of God's restoration of Job. I had always assumed God restored Job's health and wealth as soon as Job's encounter with God ended. But Job 42:10 clearly says God restored Job *after* he prayed for his friends. In looking outward to minister to others, Job experienced God's blessing.

It's all too easy to become self-absorbed when facing problems and troubles. God taught Job (and us) a valuable lesson. One way to endure problems is to look beyond ourselves to others. In ministering to others we will find the strength and endurance to handle our own struggles.

Endurance Comes from Looking Forward

Job looked inward for integrity, he looked upward for stability, and he looked outward for service. All three helped him endure. But Job looked in one additional direction . . . and it provided hope. He looked forward to the time when God would make all things right!

Job expected to die from the disease devastating his body. But Job could endure because he looked beyond this life to a life that existed beyond the grave. "I know that my Redeemer lives, and that in the end he will stand upon the earth. And after my skin has been destroyed, yet in my flesh I will see God; I myself will see him with my own eyes—I, and not another. How my heart yearns within me!" (Job 19:25–27).

Job could endure because he somehow sensed life didn't end at death. Remember, Job had none of the Bible. Based on his age and other background details he must have lived in the patriarchal period—hundreds of years before Moses penned the first books of the Bible. He did not know God's plan for the ages. He didn't comprehend the death . . . and resurrection . . . of God's Son. And he had no detailed knowledge of God's future resurrection or of the new heavens and new earth where all God's people will spend eternity.

Yet, Job instinctively knew there was more to life than just physical existence on this earth. And he knew God would one day make everything right. He could confidently state, "But he knows the way that I take; when he has tested me, I will come forth as gold" (Job 23:10). He could endure because he looked beyond his circumstances to the future.

RUN THE RACE

When I think of endurance, I think of marathon runners. Their grit, determination, and drive are worthy examples of the endurance we ought to display in our lives. The writer of Hebrews compared our spiritual life to a "race marked out for us" (Hebrews 12:1). He urged us to "run with perseverance." We need to stay the course. But what are the items on our mental checklist we must remember if we are to run with perseverance? The writer focused on the same four items that helped Job endure.

- **Look inward**—"Throw off everything that hinders and the sin that so easily entangles" (Hebrews 12:1).
- **Look upward**—"Let us fix our eyes on Jesus, the author and perfecter of our faith" (Hebrews 12:2).
- **Look outward**—"Make every effort to live in peace with all men and to be holy; . . . See to it that no one misses the grace of God" (Hebrews 12:14–15).
- **Look forward**—"Therefore, since we are receiving a kingdom that cannot be shaken, let us be thankful, and so worship God acceptably with reverence and awe" (Hebrews 12:28).

Reflect and Respond

We must view the Christian life as a marathon, not a hun-dred-meter dash. Endurance is essential for surviving the highs . . . and lows . . . of "the race marked out for us."

1. As you have read through this book, did you make any specific commitments to be a man or woman of integrity? Now is the time to look inward and reaffirm your commitment to personal integrity . . . whatever life brings your way.
2. What are the "fixed points" you are using to establish your spiritual bearings? Are your eyes fixed on Jesus? On studying His Word? On spending time with Him in prayer? Looking beyond your problems to the God who can solve your problems will help you endure.
3. Who are the people in your life now causing you the most grief? Choose one and pray for him or her this week. Ask God to provide one specific way for you to show kindness to that person. Don't become a prisoner to your anger.
4. Memorize John 14:1–4 and view your problems from an eternal perspective. The problems you face today are only temporary. Heaven is eternal.

"And we pray this in order that you may live a life worthy of the Lord and may please him in every way: bearing fruit in every good work, growing in the knowledge of God, being strengthened with all power according to his glorious might so that you may have great endurance and patience." (Colossians 1:10–11)

I BELIEVE THE SINGLE MOST
SIGNIFICANT DECISION I CAN MAKE ON
A DAY-TO-DAY BASIS IS MY CHOICE OF
ATTITUDE. WHEN MY ATTITUDES ARE
RIGHT, THERE IS NO BARRIER TOO HIGH,
NO VALLEY TOO DEEP, NO DREAM TOO
EXTREME, NO CHALLENGE TOO GREAT
FOR ME.

—*Charles R. Swindoll*

10

THE MISSING INGREDIENT:
Joy

What is a chapter on *joy* doing at the end of a book on character and integrity? Isn't joy a *feeling* while the other chapters focus on *behaviors*? Bear with me on this. I've included this chapter because I believe joy *is* an essential element of Christian character. A life of integrity produces joy, but beyond that, Christians who display joy have a profound impact on others. It is a compelling character trait that can draw others toward God.

GRUMPY OLD MAN

Everyone liked to visit Aunt Hannah, but most dreaded talking with Uncle Paul. This childless couple was the last of my father's aunts and uncles who lived nearby. Aunt Hannah reminded me of "Aunt Bea" on the Andy Griffith show. She was a warmhearted, matronly woman who prepared some of the best home-cooked meals I ever tasted—from the perfectly cooked roast to smooth gravy to the flaky crust on her home-made apple pie. Going to Aunt Hannah's for dinner was fun . . . except for Uncle Paul.

Uncle Paul was the consummate crank. By the end of his life, his major activities were describing his past indiscretions and his current physical ailments.

Dad always barked out the same warning before we went to visit Aunt Hannah and Uncle Paul. "Don't ask Uncle Paul how he feels!" That was a recipe for disaster. I know because one time I forgot and asked. His detailed description of the surgical removal of most of his stomach did wonders to my appetite . . . especially since the description lasted for most of the meal! When we left later that evening, he was still describing the various operations, ailments, and medications around which his life revolved. I never again asked him how he felt!

After I left home and moved away to college, I would still

visit Aunt Hannah and Uncle Paul when I came home. Every visit ended the same way. As I would say good-bye, Uncle Paul would come over and say, "Yea, I'd better say good-bye. I just might not be here when you get back this way again to visit." And he was not talking about moving to Maui! This lasted for fifteen years.

Uncle Paul finally died, and I went back home for the funeral. Two sad thoughts played on my mind while I was there. First, I could not recall being with Uncle Paul one single time when he was actually fun to be around. Instead, I remembered him for his self-centeredness and self-pity. Second, I wondered how many of those in attendance would have come to Uncle Paul's funeral had it not been for Aunt Hannah. More came to pay their respects to her than to honor him.

All of us know our own Uncle Pauls. One comic strip even revolves around the life of a classic, crotchety old man. It's called *Crankshaft*, and it can be brutally funny. This strip of Crankshaft and a friend in a restaurant is typical. [15]

The world seems to be full of Ed Crankshafts whose mission in life is to make everyone they meet as miserable as they are. And many do so in the name of Christ! They somehow equate a sour disposition and a furrowed brow with spiritual maturity. How sad.

When I was a boy, someone gave me a windup watch. I made sure I wound it every morning. I was always concerned the watch might wind down during the night, so I wound the spring as tight as I could every day. Unfortunately I kept the tension on the spring so tight that eventually the spring snapped and the watch quit running.

People, like watches, can also get wound too tight. And when they do, they snap.

Lives that are stressed out, frazzled, and wound too tight need a break that will provide some sense of balance. One remedy prescribed by God is joy.

LIVING *ABOVE* THE CIRCUMSTANCES

"So, Frank, how's it going?"

"Okay, under the circumstances."

Ever have that conversation? Most of us have. We see our lives and well-being tied to circumstances that swirl out of control around us. Advertisers assault us with the message that we won't find true happiness unless we purchase a new car, buy new clothes, find a new romantic interest, or make over our physique. The subtle message is that to be happy we need to change our circumstances.

If circumstances dictate happiness, how happy would you be serving a four-year prison sentence for a crime you didn't commit? Imagine how you would feel if, during that time, you watched your already shaky financial situation slip further into the red. Then imagine how you would respond to news that a very close friend who had faithfully come to visit you was ill and at the point of death. No freedom . . . no financial security . . . no way to help a friend in need. *Under the circumstances* you might be discouraged and depressed. But the one who faced these problems was not "under the circumstances" . . . he lived *above* them. He was the apostle Paul.

The Jewish religious leaders attacked Paul in Jerusalem during a visit to the temple (Acts 21). The Roman garrison that arrested him actually saved his life by rescuing him from a mob planning to stone him to death. The religious leaders lodged trumped-up charges against Paul, and he spent two years awaiting trial at the coastal city of Caesarea (Acts 23:33–35; 24:27). After two years the religious leaders asked to have Paul brought back to Jerusalem, but they planned to ambush the garrison along the way and kill Paul. Exercising his rights as a Roman citizen, Paul appealed to Caesar to have his case decided in Rome. After a hair-raising voyage across the Mediterranean (including a shipwreck on Malta), Paul arrived in Rome only to spend another two years under house arrest awaiting the arrival of his accusers. Paul lost four years of his life for a crime he never committed. *Under the circumstances* we could expect Paul to become bitter and disillusioned, but he wouldn't!

Rome had a unique plan to control prison overpopulation and lower the cost of maintaining their prison system. The Roman authorities allowed some prisoners to live in homes under "house arrest." The prisoner was responsible to pay for his housing and meals, but he was not allowed to leave the home to work. (In fact, he was chained to a Roman guard during this imprisonment!) Paul was given the privilege of being under house arrest (Acts 28:16, 30). He could receive visitors, meet with close friends, and correspond freely with those in other cities. The main problem facing Paul was getting the money to pay for the house!

In the best of times Paul received adequate finances for his ministry. He could work as a tentmaker, and some churches sent financial contributions to help fund his work. But at other times the work disappeared and the financial contributions dried up. Paul knew the best—and worst—of financial times. "I know what it is to be in need, and I know what it is to have plenty," he wrote. The breadth of situations faced by Paul included being "well fed or hungry . . . living in plenty or in want" (Philippians 4:12). Unable to work while confined to house arrest . . . responsible for his own lodging and living expenses . . . receiving little financial support from churches where he had labored so diligently. *Under the circumstances* we could expect Paul to be discouraged. But he wasn't!

A gift finally arrived from the church in Philippi. Hand-carried by a personal friend of Paul, the gift was as refreshing as a cold drink of water on a hot day. But that brief moment of happiness was shattered when Epaphroditus, this courier and friend, fell ill. All Paul's prayers and all Dr. Luke's medical skills seemed unable to stop the illness that wrapped its arms around Epaphroditus and pulled him ever closer to the abyss of death. *Under the circumstances* we could expect Paul to be disheartened and give up. But he didn't!

> SOMETIMES IT'S EASIER TO TRUST GOD FOR WHAT HE WILL DO IN OTHERS' LIVES THAN IT IS TO TRUST HIM TO WORK IN OUR OWN.

Pen in hand, Paul sat down to write to the congregation that had shared so generously with him. Chains clanking as he shuffled around the room, Paul dictated one of the most upbeat letters found in the New Testament—the epistle to the Philippians. *Under the circumstances* we wouldn't expect Paul to focus on the theme of joy. But he did!

Rejoice in the Lord Always!

How could Paul ever find such joy in the problems he faced? The church in Philippi must have wondered how Paul could survive emotionally the many persecutions, trials, and injustices he had undergone. Imagine their surprise when they received his heartening letter!

Paul's ability to experience joy was to look beyond his circumstances to the Lord. Problems come and go. Circumstances constantly change. But God is unchangeable and His plan is unalterable. Looking to God can provide stability and hope . . . and this leads to joy.

Paul began his letter by sharing the secret for his great confidence and joy. "I thank my God every time I remember you. . . . I always pray with joy . . . being confident of this, that he who began a good work in you will carry it on to completion until the day of Christ Jesus" (Philippians 1:3–6). Paul wasn't wringing his hands in emotional agony over what would happen to these churches in his absence. God was in charge, and he could depend on God to work everything out.

And yet, sometimes it's easier to trust God for what He will do in others' lives than it is to trust Him to work in our own. How can we be joyful when we are being personally attacked, maligned, and misunderstood? We can almost hear Paul's friends in Philippi whisper this question to themselves. After all, there were some scoundrels in Rome preaching in the name of Christ just to cause problems for Paul. And Paul could do nothing to stop them. Would he be discouraged, angry, perhaps even bitter over this gross injustice? Not Paul!

"But what does it matter? The important thing is that in every way, whether from false motives or true, Christ is preached. And because of this I rejoice. Yes, and I will continue to rejoice, . . . For to me, to live is Christ and to die is gain" (Philippians 1:18, 21). Instead of being discouraged,

Paul was *excited* about those preaching Christ to cause him trouble.

"Look at the big picture!" he told his readers. "More people are sharing Christ than ever before!"

But what if they cause so much trouble you are put to death? "If I die, I win! I'll be with Christ in heaven forever!"

Paul was joyful because he viewed his circumstance from God's perspective. He wasn't *under the circumstances*, he was looking above them to see what God was doing.

Paul seems to stress two themes relating to the joy he had in the Lord. The first is the fact that he could rejoice because he knew the Lord was in charge. He saw the hand of God in everything taking place—even those events that caused him temporary discomfort or difficulty. Thus he could take his concerns to the Lord and trust the Lord to work them out. Paul's second theme is the fact he knew the Lord could return at any time. His problems were just temporary inconveniences that would soon be replaced by permanent fellowship with the Lord.

Both themes join together in Paul's exhortation to live lives of joyful expectation and trust.

> *"Rejoice in the Lord always. I will say it again: Rejoice! Let your gentleness be evident to all. The Lord is near. Do not be anxious about anything, but in everything, by prayer and petition, with thanksgiving, present your requests to God. And the peace of God, which transcends all understanding, will guard your hearts and your minds in Christ Jesus."* (Philippians 4:4–7)

Paul experienced joy and a sense of freedom in spite of his circumstances because he knew the Lord was near . . . and watching. He could face life with confidence because he understood the power and presence of God.

Rejoice in Serving Others

When I was a young child, a Sunday school teacher taught me a way to "J-O-Y" in the Christian life: Jesus first, Others second, Yourself last. Paul didn't know that jingle, but he understood the concept. Much of his joy came from putting the Lord first in his life and viewing life from God's perspective. But Paul also understood the second principle that would lead to joy—putting others ahead of ourselves.

Pausing to choose his words carefully, Paul boldly asked the Philippians to make his joy complete "by being like-minded, having the same love, being one in spirit and purpose." This would require them to "do nothing out of selfish ambition or vain conceit, but in humility consider others better than yourselves" (Philippians 2:2–3).

Some of the saddest individuals alive today are people who think only of themselves. Their lives are so self-absorbed they have no understanding of the personal satisfaction they can experience through serving others.

Paul realized the best way to teach the people of Philippi this truth was to wrap it in human form. We learn best when we can observe specific examples. As the old saying goes, "Some things are better caught than taught." Paul provided four specific examples of individuals who found joy in serving others.

Jesus

The apostle used Jesus as his first example. "Your attitude should be the same as that of Christ Jesus" (Philippians 2:5). Jesus was willing to give up His rightful place in heaven to lay aside His glory and become a man. As the God-man He took on the role of a servant and willingly gave His life on the cross to purchase eternal life for others. In arguing from the greater to the lesser Paul emphasized that if the Son of God was willing to give up His rightful place in heaven to serve us, we ought to be willing to give up some of our "rights" to serve others.

Paul

Most—perhaps all—of Paul's readers had never met Jesus during His time on earth. Certainly they knew what Jesus had done. For the "joy set before him" Jesus had "endured the cross" (Hebrews 12:2). He hadn't come to earth "to be served, but to serve" (Matthew 20:28). But some may have had trouble relating to His example because Jesus was the perfect God-man while they struggled as "mere mortals." As if anticipating their objection, Paul moved quickly to his second example . . . himself!

Paul urged his readers to "do everything without complaining or arguing" (Philippians 2:14). They were to be different from the rest of society. Living in the midst of the "crooked and depraved generation" of their day, individuals who could display joyful contentment would "shine like stars" (2:15). Paul then used his own response to his four-year imprisonment as an example for them to follow. His willingness to share God's good news with individuals like those in Philippi had put him in prison, on trial for his very life. "But even if I am being poured out like a drink offering on the sacrifice and service coming from your faith, I am glad and rejoice with all of you" (2:17). Service for others brought joy.

HIS WILLINGNESS TO SHARE GOD'S GOOD NEWS WITH INDIVIDUALS LIKE THOSE IN PHILIPPI HAD PUT HIM IN PRISON, ON TRIAL FOR HIS VERY LIFE.

Timothy

Paul's third example was his protégé, Timothy. Timothy remembered Philippi well! After joining Paul early in his second missionary journey (Acts 16:1–3), Timothy sailed with Paul from Asia Minor to Europe. Philippi was the first European city where Paul planted a church (Acts 16:12–40). Timothy experienced the early revival, the Satanic opposition, the unruly mob, and the ugly beating and imprisonment. He also shook with the force of the earthquake that rocked the city and sprang open the door of the jail holding Paul and Silas. Sometime later Paul sent Timothy and another disciple back to Philippi as his special envoys (Acts 19:21–22). The Philippians knew Timothy!

Paul introduced this example by expressing his desire to send Timothy to Philippi on a fact-finding mission. But then the masterful teacher explained why he was so eager to send Timothy. "I have no one else like him, who takes a genuine interest in your welfare. For everyone looks out for his own interests, not those of Jesus Christ. But you know that Timothy has proved himself . . ." (Philippians 2:20–22a). In effect, Paul says to the Philippians, "Want a third example of selfless service for others? Think back and remember how Timothy conducted himself when he was with you!"

Paul stresses three specific concerns that consumed Timothy. Timothy took a "genuine interest" in the welfare of the church at Philippi (2:20). Timothy also focused on the interests of Jesus Christ (2:21), and as a dutiful son he willingly served with Paul (2:22). The one area Timothy did *not* make a priority was "his own interests" (2:21). Timothy had shown the Philippians how to spell "JOY": Jesus first; Others second; Yourself last.

Epaphroditus

Paul's gallery of godly examples has been impressive. Jesus, Paul himself, and Timothy. But Paul saved the most visible example for last. Paul's letter to the Philippians was hand-carried by Epaphroditus—one of their own members. The church in Philippi had sent Epaphroditus on a "mission of mercy" to Paul in Rome. Along with kind words of greeting, this trusted messenger also carried a sizable offering from the church to help Paul with his living expenses during his time in prison.

Epaphroditus's kind actions almost turned to tragedy when he fell deathly ill during his stay in Rome. Paul pulled no punches in describing the gravity of the situation. "Indeed he was ill, and almost died" (Philippians 2:27). What caused this serious illness? Paul does not say specifically, but he implies the illness resulted, in some measure, from his ministry to Paul. Epaphroditus "almost died for the work of Christ, risking his life to make up for the help you could not give me" (2:30).

I imagine Epaphroditus blushed when the letter was read aloud in the church and Paul singled him out by name. This unpretentious servant became more distressed over learning his home church heard "he was ill" than he had been over the illness! Paul stresses the same three priorities in Epaphroditus that he had earlier used for Timothy. Epaphroditus focused on doing "the work of Christ," on making a hazardous journey from Philippi to Rome to "take care of [Paul's] needs," and on serving as the "messenger" from Philippi who could "make up for the help you could not give me." Epaphroditus could also show the Philippians how to spell "JOY": Jesus first; Others second; Yourself last.

Reflect and Respond

The old saying is still true: JOY is spelled Jesus first, Others second, and Yourself last. Love Jesus, look for ways to serve others . . . and laugh!

1. Are there any specific problems or circumstances that seem to be sucking the joy from your life right now? If so, make a list of them. Can you trust Jesus to take care of all those problems? Pray over your list and ask the Lord to help you see your problems from His perspective . . . to take you above your circumstances.
2. How are you serving others in your church or community? Plan one project you can do this week to help someone less fortunate than yourself.
3. When was the last time you laughed so hard you started to cry? What were you doing? Who was there? Call that person and tell them you were just thinking about a great time you once had together and wanted to call and share it again. Relive the experience with your friend . . . and laugh!
4. Memorize Philippians 4:4 and ask God to let your life reflect His joy.

"A cheerful heart is good medicine, but a crushed spirit dries up the bones." (Proverbs 17:22)

IF YOU CAN'T FEED A HUNDRED PEOPLE,
THEN FEED JUST ONE.

—*Mother Teresa*

11

CAN ONE PERSON MAKE A
Difference?

My family traces its roots back to colonial New England. Decades ago an aging member of the family, Jinks Dyer (his real name!), sat down and wrote out all the traditions and history that had been passed down to him by parents, grandparents, aunts, and uncles. I received a copy of this handwritten history, and I found it to be fascinating . . . skeletons and all!

The first Dyers to come to America, William and Mary Dyer, landed at Boston in 1635. The family background of William and Mary remains shrouded in mystery. Tradition says that Mary Dyer was the only daughter of Sir William Seymour and Arabella Stuart, cousin of King James I of England. The King felt threatened by this marriage and had William Seymour and Arabella imprisoned in the Tower of London. Their child was secretly raised by Arabella's lady-in-waiting, Mary Dyer, who gave her name to the infant girl. Quite a story! But it gets even better.

Boston in 1635 was a bastion of Puritan worship and law. The Puritans fled to America to seek religious freedom, but they refused to extend that freedom to other religious groups. William and Mary Dyer ran afoul of the authorities when they sided with those who taught salvation by grace rather than salvation by works. Forced to leave Boston, they traveled west to a settlement started two years earlier by Roger Williams. That settlement, in what is today Rhode Island, offered William and Mary the opportunity for religious freedom.

Mary Dyer's spiritual pilgrimage continued until she met George Fox, who persuaded her to become a Quaker. From that time on, Mary felt compelled to return to Boston to be a witness to that closed community. Twice she returned to Boston. Both times she was arrested. Her life reads like a tragic novel. Imprisoned, banished, imprisoned again, and finally tried and sentenced to death by hanging.

From the jail where she would one day be led out to be

hanged, Mary wrote to the Boston magistrates, "My life not availeth me in comparison to the liberty of the truth." Those words are now inscribed on a bronze statue of Mary Dyer that stands in front of the Massachusetts state capitol in Boston. Mary Dyer passionately believed in the truth of those words, and she willingly gave her life for that truth. But was her life in vain?

Ruth Plimpton records the aftermath of Mary Dyer's death . . . and the effect it had on one of the spectators who witnessed her execution.

> Edward Wanton vomited in Frog Pond three times before he could mount his steed. As he trotted past the great elm tree, his horse whinnied, reared, and almost threw him to the ground. He pressed his heels and hurried home. Once inside his mother's house, he threw down his musket and halberd. Sinking his head in his arms he sobbed, "Alas Mother! We have been murdering the Lord's people," and taking off his sword, he made a vow never to wear it again. Not long after, he became a member of the Society of Friends and two years later he was arrested for holding Quaker meetings in his house. [16]

WHAT DIFFERENCE DOES ONE LIFE MAKE?

Can one person make a difference? Yes, if that individual is a man or woman of integrity. If that individual shines as a light in a dark world. If that individual displays the character of Jesus Christ in word . . . and deed. God specializes in changing the world one person at a time.

The prophet Micah lived in dark days. Corruption and compromise marked the nation of Judah. "Her leaders judge for a bribe, her priests teach for a price, and her prophets tell fortunes for money" (Micah 3:11). The nation careened out of control, plunging down a treacherous path that could end only in catastrophe. "Therefore because of you, Zion will be plowed like a field, Jerusalem will become a heap of rubble, the temple hill a mound overgrown with thickets" (Micah 3:12).

Yet God called Micah to be different . . . to stand as a model of integrity and righteousness. After describing society's moral cesspool, Micah announced his willingness to stand alone for the truth. "But as for me, I am filled with power, with the Spirit of the Lord, and with justice and might, to declare to Jacob his transgression, to Israel his sin" (Micah 3:8).

But what can one person do alone? How can one individual make a difference? Micah doesn't provide the answer, but another prophet does. A century after Micah, Jeremiah the prophet also stood alone to face a nation collectively spitting in the face of God. On one particular occasion Jeremiah delivered an impassioned message to those gathered in the temple in Jerusalem. When he finished, a crowd seized him and screamed, "You must die!" (Jeremiah 26:8). Many expected a swift trial . . . and certain death. But some of the elders stepped forward to defend Jeremiah. They compared his words to those spoken a century earlier by Micah.

"Some of the elders of the land stepped forward and said to the entire assembly of people, 'Micah of Moresheth prophesied in the days of Hezekiah king of Judah. He told all the people of Judah, "This is what the Lord Almighty says"'" (Jeremiah 26:17–18). Micah's words stood the test of time. People remembered the message long after Micah was gone. But Micah's prophecies had done more than merely fill heads with knowledge. Micah single-handedly changed an entire generation!

After quoting Micah's prophecy of judgment (Micah 3:12), the elders reminded the mob of the impact Micah's message had made on the people to whom he spoke. "Did Hezekiah king of Judah or anyone else in Judah put him to death? Did not Hezekiah fear the Lord and seek his favor? And did not the Lord relent, so that he did not bring the disaster he pronounced against them? We are about to bring a terrible disaster on ourselves!" (Jeremiah 26:19).

Micah may have stood alone, but his message had an impact on his nation! Micah's willingness to stand for what was right . . . to swim against the current . . . changed an entire generation. God held back His judgment because a nation repented in response to Micah's words and deeds. One man made a difference!

WHERE DO I GO FROM HERE?

Life brings change. Where you live. Where you work. How you dress. All these can, and often do, change over time. Flexibility and adaptability are two traits that can help us respond to the accelerating rate of change taking place all around us.

But some things must never change. Integrity should never go out of style. Christlike character remains God's standard for those who claim His Son as their Savior. Your commitment to a lifestyle patterned after Jesus Christ must never waver.

The world offers "the good life," God gives eternal life. The world emphasizes "doing," God emphasizes "being." The world stresses achievement, God stresses integrity. The world pressures to conform, God seeks to transform. The world focuses on the outward signs of "success," God focuses on the inner qualities of the heart.

Like a skilled physician, Chuck Swindoll looked past the symptoms to diagnose the true problem.

As I wade through the success propaganda written today, again and again the focus of attention is on one's outer self— how smart I can appear, what a good impression I can make, how much I can own or how totally I can control or how fast I can be promoted or . . . or . . . or. Nothing I read—and I mean *nothing*—places emphasis on the heart, the inner being, the seed plot of our thoughts, motives, decisions. Nothing, that is, except Scripture.

Interestingly, the Bible says little about success, but a lot about the heart, the place where true success originates. [17]

Think of this book as a spiritual "stress test." Throughout the book you have been experiencing God's treadmill of integrity. God has been monitoring all your spiritual vital signs, checking for any irregularities. Back in the Great Physician's office, you hear the diagnosis . . . and prognosis.

The Great Physician notes areas of strength . . . and weakness. Some lifestyle changes are necessary for complete spiritual health. But now the book is finished . . . the examination is over. As you walk from the office, you know that the decision to change, or not to change, is one that only you can make.

William Longstaff, an English businessman, made a decision to live a life of integrity and holiness. He wrote down on paper a simple poem explaining what living such a life meant to him . . . and years later his poem, "Take Time to Be Holy," was set to music. As William and Randy Petersen discovered, this simple poem "may have been the only poem he ever wrote. . . . A businessman at heart, Longstaff wrote no flowery or pious-sounding verses, but these down-to-earth thoughts." [18]

Read Longstaff's words carefully . . . and make them your own as you decide *now* to live a life of integrity.

"Take Time to Be Holy"

Take time to be holy, speak oft with thy Lord;
Abide in Him always, and feed on His Word.
Make friends of God's children; help those who are weak;
Forgetting in nothing His blessing to seek.

Take time to be holy, the world rushes on;
Much time spend in secret with Jesus alone;
By looking to Jesus, like Him thou shalt be;
Thy friends in thy conduct His likeness shall see.

Take time to be holy, let Him be thy guide,
And run not before Him whatever betide;
In joy or in sorrow still follow thy Lord,
And, looking to Jesus, still trust in His Word.

Take time to be holy, be calm in thy soul;
Each thought and each motive beneath His control;
Thus led by His Spirit to fountains of love,
Thou soon shalt be fitted for service above.

NOTES

Why Talk about Character?

1. http://www.washingtonpost.com/wp-dyn/content/article/2008/12/12/AR 2008121203970.html
2. "Ryan convicted in corruption trial," *Chicago Tribune*, April 17, 2006.
3. Charles Dyer, *The Power of Personal Integrity* (Carol Stream, Ill.: Tyndale, 1997).
4. *Newsweek*, April 13, 2009.
5. Ibid., 34.

Chapter 1: Under the Lamplight: Honesty

6. Jon Winokur, ed., *The Portable Curmudgeon* (New York: Penguin Books, 1987), 69.
7. http://www.willrogers.com/says/will_says.html
8. http://www.quotationspage.com/quote/24939.html
9. Amanda Paulson, "Corruption winds through Illinois politics," *The Christian Science Monitor*, December 11, 2008.
10. Rod Handley, "Leaving a Distinctive Mark: Building a Legacy of Character, Integrity, and Accountability," *Outcomes* (Summer 2009), 26.

Chapter 2: Widows and Wheatfields: Compassion

11. Bob St. John, "Slip of the ears can leave you embarrassed," *Dallas Morning News*, March 5, 1989, A37.

Chapter 4: By-laws or Bye, Laws?: Self-control

12. Stephen R. Covey, *The 7 Habits of Highly Effective People* (New York: Simon & Schuster, 1989), 92.

Chapter 9: Lacking Nothing: Endurance

13. Bertha Spafford Vester, *Our Jerusalem*, reprint ed. (Jerusalem: Ariel Publishing House, 1988), 47.

14. These are the handwritten words as they appear on the stationery of the Brevoort House hotel . . . the first draft of Spafford's poem. Spafford modified the words slightly when the poem was set to music. The most significant change was the final line, which was changed to " 'Even so'— it is well with my soul" to continue the theme of Christ's second coming.

Chapter 10: The Missing Ingredient: Joy

15. *Crankshaft* (new) © 2009 Mediagraphics, Inc. North America syndicate. Used with permission.

Chapter 11: Can One Person Make a Difference?

16. Ruth Plimpton, *Mary Dyer: Biography of a Rebel Quaker* (Boston: Branden Publishing Co., 1994), 188–89.

17. Charles R. Swindoll, *The Quest for Character* (Grand Rapids: Zondervan, 1982), 27.

18. William J. Petersen and Randy Petersen provide the background for this hymn in their devotional for May 31 in *The One Year Book of Hymns*, edited by Robert K. Brown and Mark R. Norton (Wheaton, Ill.: Tyndale House Publishers, 1995).

ISBN-13: 978-0-8024-2908-7

A VOICE
in the
WILDERNESS

"The Bible is not a sterile Book immaculately conceived in some sort of mystical, holy vacuum. Though God is the ultimate Author, He used human writers as His instruments. And to properly interpret His Word we must enter their world. The bleating of sheep on barren hills, the mournful wail of a ram's horn trumpet on the temple steps, the harsh clang of sword hitting sword in epic battle hang like tapestries in the background of every page."

Life's struggles can make us feel as if we're wandering in the desert, thirsty for hope and healing. Using Isaiah 40 as a backdrop, bestselling author Charles Dyer takes us on a journey through ancient Judea for a vivid reminder that others before us have known suffering—and, just as God was present for them in their pain, He will walk with us through our wilderness.

Charles H. dyer

MOODY
PUBLISHERS

MoodyPublishers.com

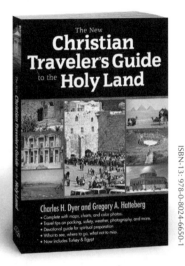

ISBN-13: 978-0-8024-6650-1

The New
Christian
Traveler's Guide
to the Holy Land

Knowing the Land helps us understand the Book in new and vivid ways. Charles Dyer, a Bible scholar and licensed tour guide for Israel, and Greg Hatteberg, graduate of the Institute of Holy Land Studies in Jerusalem, created this reference guide for pilgrims who want to deepen the spiritual impact of their trip to Israel, as well as other travelers who just want to know more: where did Jesus walk? what happened in Jerusalem? why is Petra important? You'll find detailed information about five key Bible lands: Israel, Egypt, Greece, Jordan, and Turkey. This guide includes a full color 32-page photo insert, practical tips for travelers, a 4-week prayer guide for preparing for your trip, and detailed maps and an outline of Bible history. With *The New Christian Traveler's Guide to the Holy Land*, you'll see the Bible through a new set of geographical lenses.

Charles H. Dyer | Gregory A. Hatteberg

MOODY
PUBLISHERS

MoodyPublishers.com

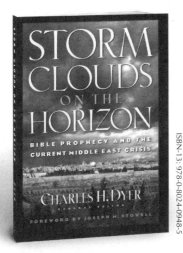

ISBN-13: 978-0-8024-0948-5

STORM
CLOUDS
ON THE
HORIZON

You hear news stories daily about important events taking place in the Middle East. But do you fully comprehend what's going on in Israel? Do you understand the significance those events have for your own life? Find out what's happening in the Middle East today and learn how those events are linked to key biblical prophecies.

• Why is Israel constantly in the news today?
• What does the Bible say about Israel's past and future?
• How does God's plan for the church differ from His plan for Israel?
• Why can't the United Nations bring peace to the earth?
• Is the United States mentioned in Bible prophecy?

CHARLES H. DYER

MOODY
PUBLISHERS

MoodyPublishers.com

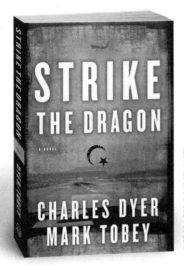

ISBN-13: 978-0-8024-3908-6

STRIKE
THE DRAGON

A cell phone awakens a young mother in a Palestinian refugee camp. The simple message, "It is time," jolts her awake. Dressing in clothes that once belonged to her dead husband, she asks her mother to watch her young son. Upon arriving at the mosque she meets the man who had called. He takes her to two other men who will transport her, and the bomb she will wear, to the proper destination—the West Bank city of Ariel. A story of international terrorism and intrigue unfolds across the globe. Special agents and covert operatives track clues to pinpoint the probability of an attack that will dwarf previous attempts to strike where it hurts the most.

CHARLES DYER I MARK TOBEY

MOODY
PUBLISHERS

MoodyPublishers.com